THINK LIKE
A TITAN

Lessons from Jeff Bezos, Bill Gates, and Warren Buffett

By Andrew Adams

© **Copyright 2019 - All rights reserved.**

The content contained within this book may not be reproduced, duplicated or transmitted without direct written permission from the author or the publisher.

Under no circumstances will any blame or legal responsibility be held against the publisher, or author for any damages, reparation, or monetary loss due to the information contained within this book, either directly or indirectly.

Legal Notice:

This book is copyright protected. This book is only for personal use. You cannot amend, distribute, sell, use, quote or paraphrase any part, or the content within this book, without the consent of the author or publisher.

Disclaimer Notice:

Please note the information contained within this document is for educational and entertainment purposes only. All effort has been executed to present accurate, up to date, reliable, and complete information. No warranties of any kind are declared or implied. Readers acknowledge that the author is not engaging in the rendering of legal, financial, medical or professional advice. The content within this book has been derived from various sources. Please consult a licensed professional before attempting any techniques outlined in this book.

By reading this document, the reader agrees that under no circumstances is the author responsible for any losses, direct or indirect, which are incurred as a result of the use of information contained within this document, including but not limited to, — errors, omissions, or inaccuracies.

Table of Contents

JEFF BEZOS 5

   Introduction 6

   CHAPTER 1: The Business Titan 8

   CHAPTER 2: Titans Are Risk Takers 10

   CHAPTER 3: Focus on the Customer 17

   CHAPTER 4: Adopting a Good Name 28

   CHAPTER 5: Invest More on the Product 32

   CHAPTER 6: Sell Premium Products at Nonpremium Prices 38

   CHAPTER 7: Build a Culture 40

   CHAPTER 8: The Importance of Frugal Thinking 47

   CHAPTER 9: Surround Yourself with the Right People 53

   CHAPTER 10: Long-Term Thinking 58

   Conclusion 61

BILL GATES 63

   Introduction 64

   CHAPTER 1: Learning the Art of Success in Business 66

   CHAPTER 2: 10 Commandments for Succeeding in Business 74

   CHAPTER 3: Rules for Success from Bill Gates 81

   CHAPTER 4: Critical Factors that Determine the Success of a Business 98

   Final Thoughts (Conclusion) 103

WARREN BUFFETT 107

   Introduction and a short Bio 108

CHAPTER 1: Famous Quotes by Warren Buffett 117

CHAPTER 2: Warren Buffett's Rules for Success 120

CHAPTER 3: Other Success Rules of Warren Buffett 129

CHAPTER 4: Facts about Warren Buffett's Investment Lessons ... 133

CHAPTER 5: Value Investing Tips by Warren Buffett 139

CHAPTER 6: Warren Buffett's Investing Style 145

CHAPTER 7: Why Warren Buffett should be your role model 150

Conclusion 155

JEFF BEZOS

Introduction

Developing the mindset of a business titan is not something you achieve in a single day. It takes years of practice to completely refine your thought processes to align with that of a business titan. Nonetheless, following in the footsteps of a business titan can help you correctly develop this mindset in a short time.

Jeff Bezos (Amazon founder and CEO) is arguably one of the greatest business titans in the world today. As the wealthiest man in the world, there are various principles he followed to ensure the growth and success of his business.

There are various principles that Jeff Bezos usually focuses on when writing his annual letters. Some of these principles include focusing on the customers, building a culture, taking risks, long-term thinking, building the right team, and many more. Over the years, these letters have offered insights into his life.

This book is an important piece in helping you understand some of the most important principles in his annual letters. From this book, you will take away a mindset that will set you apart as a business titan.

Nothing is ever easy. The best things in life are open to you after a lot of challenges and failure. The mindset of a business titan is the only way through which you can rise above these challenges and failures.

Success is a process; you cannot rush it. The journey of a thousand miles begins with a step. It is the first step you need to take.

CHAPTER 1: The Business Titan

Who Is a Business Titan?

A business titan is a person who is very successful in the business industry. As the founder and CEO of Amazon, Jeff Bezos is a business titan in the retail internet industry.

Do You Have to Be a Business Titan to Think Like One?

You do not have to be a business titan to think like one. A business titan is only used to refer to a person who is very influential in the business world. They are individuals whose success is known to the whole world.

Every business owner wants to become a business titan at one point or another. The truth is that this is possible. All it takes is time, the right mindset, and a proper business strategy.

Thinking like a business titan is not as easy as you may think. It takes time to rigorously train yourself to develop the mindset of a business titan.

The Means to Thinking like a Business Titan

There are a lot of things you can learn how to do with practice. The same applies when developing the mindset of a business titan. It is possible to learn how to think like a business titan by following the principles of your favorite business titan.

Your ability to think like a business titan is what makes an excellent entrepreneur. It is why Amazon is still experiencing massive growth even after so many years.

To think like a business titan, you have to be adaptable. Your ability to adapt is vital to emulate the thought process of a business titan.

CHAPTER 2: Titans Are Risk Takers

If you decide that you're going to do only the things you know are going to work, you're going to leave a lot of opportunity on the table.

—*Jeff Bezos, Amazon founder and CEO*

The first step to becoming a business titan is to become a risk taker. It is the only way you will be able to grab the many opportunities lying in front of you.

Jeff Bezos is an individual who understands the importance of taking risks. Over the years, Amazon has experienced few failures when implementing new, different ideas. However, their successes are numerous. Most risks Amazon has taken have paved the way for more profitable ventures.

One of the most notable risks Amazon has taken is the "Marketplace" feature. The first step Amazon took was to create Amazon Auctions. People who knew about Amazon Auctions can attest to the similarity of this platform to the eBay model. It later transformed into zShops. Later, it would become the success we now know as the Amazon Marketplace, but only after the third attempt.

Your ability to learn from your mistakes increases your likelihood of success.

Risk-Taking as a Building Block of a Business Titan

If you want to develop the mindset of a business titan, then you have to be ready to take a lot of risks. A business titan is also inherently an entrepreneur. Risk-taking is the backbone of a successful entrepreneur.

Some of the risks you'll be taking include forfeiting a stable income for up to a year, putting your name on the line for a new initiative, and investing your personal funds as capital in a new business start-up.

Moving forward, there is a certain degree of risk with every decision you make. Some of these decisions include the following:

- Implementing some changes that may cause a rift between you and your top client
- A new lead generation strategy that is ineffective
- Hiring a new employee who may decide to leave in two weeks

Once you decide to train yourself to think like a business titan, then you should know that risks are a part of the process.

Types of Risks

Risks are in different forms, including the small and big risks. The types of risk we are more interested in are the calculable risks and ambiguous risks. Having a better understanding of the various types of risks can help in the decision-making process.

Calculable Risks

Calculable risk consists of some knowns, which enable the prediction of the possibility of success to a degree of certainty. Consider customer purchase during the Christmas season. You can use historical data to predict the chance of a 40 percent rise in profits for the sales of decorative trees.

Ambiguous Risks

In addition to some knowns, this type of risk also includes some unknowns. Including these unknowns make the decision-making more difficult. Due to various factors, like economic shifts and consumer behavior, which are not easily predictable, most business risks are ambiguous risks.

Why Risk Is a Differentiator

The impacts of risks can vary. There are certain risks with consequences that may be smaller than other risks. Some of the risks that you take can be the deciding factor on the success or failure of your business.

In business, a term that is thrown around very often is *a key differentiator*. It is a unique value that a business possesses that makes it stand out.

To a business titan, we can liken risk-taking to key

differentiators. A lot of business titans stand out from the crown due to their willingness to take risks. In the end, risk-taking can also create more opportunities in the long run.

Accept That Some of Your Risks Won't Pay Off

When talking about risks, nothing is 100 percent certain. Regarding risks, a success rate of 50 percent is a great odd while a risk that offers an 80 percent success rate is an excellent opportunity. Although we are made to believe that it is advantageous to take risks, it doesn't always yield the right results.

It is essential to accept the fact that some of your risks are going to fail. These include some of the risks that have been calculated. It is a fact you have to embrace.

Accept the likelihood of failure. If a situation arises where you fail, don't dwell on it but make sure you gain something out of the experience.

Experimentation and Failures

Experimentation is a significant reason for the success of Amazon. It is crucial you understand that most of these experiments don't always turn into a success. According to Jeff Bezos, "it's not an experiment if you know it's going to work."

Some Amazon projects that were massive failures include the following:

Music Importer

In 2012, the Music Importer was launched to allow users to create an online library by uploading their downloaded songs. This innovation would later become obsolete after company developed Prime Music.

Fire Phone

The Fire Phone was officially released in 2014 by Amazon. What the company didn't bank on was the grip that Androids and iPhones had on the market. Reducing the price of the phone to 99 cents didn't have any effect on the market. Amazon pulled the plug on the Fire Phone with a $170 million loss.

Other examples include the following:

- Amazon Destinations
- Amazon Wallet
- Amazon WebPay

What Does This Tell Us about a Business Titan?

They understand that the market evolves. In the case of the Music Importer, Jeff Bezos understood that the market was changing. Customers were becoming more interested in music streaming services, so he took a risk that paid off by offering Prime Music.

They know when to pull the plug. Learning to admit when you fail is an essential factor is becoming a great business titan. If you are unwilling to do so, you may end up with more losses than you should. In the case of the Fire Phone, Jeff Bezos had to accept its failure to mitigate the losses.

How Mistakes Can Be Helpful

As a student in school, failure often has a very negative impact. In reality, highly successful individuals all have a long history of failures. What makes these individuals different? They all ensure they can learn from these failures. According to Jeff Bezos, you cannot separate failure from innovation.

How Does Failure Create the Mindset of a Business Titan?

Failure creates humility. A valuable lesson that you can learn from failure is humility. By learning humility, it becomes easy to understand that you still have a lot of room to improve.

Wisdom stems from failures. When you try a particular approach that fails, you learn about an idea that won't work. That is the importance of failure. When you try out different ideas, you can gather ideas that can pave the path to success.

Failure promotes flexibility. Failure is a strong factor that causes people to change their minds quickly. A lot of business titans need to be flexible to avoid failures when implementing a new idea. There are some beliefs that may be wrong. You need to be able to change such beliefs.

How Do You Embrace Your Failures?

Once you make a habit of admitting your failures, then the next step is to embrace your failure. A lot of successful individuals are defined by how they embrace their failures. For certain individuals, embracing failure is a sign of weakness. To embrace failure, some individuals describe themselves as failures. In both cases, these are negative ways of embracing failures.

Although it is the only way to gain from your failures, positively embracing failures can be a great task. An individual who can embrace failure positively can remain humble and realize that there is a need for improvement.

Learning to embrace failure is one of the main reasons why Jeff Bezos can take much greater risks. When you learn to embrace failure, you eliminate the fear of failure.

CHAPTER 3: Focus on the Customer

We see our customers as invited guests to a party, and we are the hosts. It's our job every day to make every important aspect of the customer experience a little bit better.

—*Jeff Bezos, Amazon founder and CEO*

Jeff Bezos believes that the customer should be your priority. In addition to meeting the demands of the customer, you also need to provide an experience that they cannot get from your competitors.

According to Jeff Bezos, focusing on your competitors will stop you from pioneering any new idea. Amazon has been able to offer excellent customer experience by providing what the customers need.

The introduction of the Amazon Web Services (AWS) business is a pioneering idea that Amazon developed after listening to its customers. The AWS business offers content delivery, database, storage, computing power, and other functionalities. Since it is a cloud platform, it is a lot cheaper for companies to use.

As a business titan, you should be looking to build a company that is customer-centric.

What Is a Customer-Centric Business?

It is a business that focuses on the needs of the customer when developing new products. As a result, these businesses foresee the needs of the consumers and offer products that will improve their experience.

What Makes Your Business Customer-Centric?

The way your business operates tells a lot on whether it is customer-centric or not. Below are some noticeable practices of a customer-centric brand:

- The development of products and services by a customer-centric brand focuses on the wants and needs of a customer.
- These businesses believe that you should put the customer first. They are of the belief that the brand will not survive without the customers.
- The strategies that customer-centric businesses implement are prepared with the aim of attracting and retaining loyal and profitable customers.
- The main focus of the business is to improve the customer experience through relationship building.

Why Building Trust with Customers Is Important to Your Business

There is a common belief that a business that is unable to earn the customers' trust is not going to be successful. There are a lot of reasons for this belief. One of the main reasons is that the failure to form a relationship with customers will result in loss of potential sales. There are also lots of benefits a business enjoys if it can earn the loyalty and confidence of customers. One of such benefits is the opportunity to increase product prices. Customers are going to believe in your company and remain loyal if you offer high-quality products and services.

What should you do as a business titan?

Customers can easily connect to a business that has taken a positive step toward humanizing itself. It may be through company update e-mails or newsletters. It is harder for a customer to leave a business if they can associate a face with the business.

There are other means of developing customer loyalty, including customer rewards programs.

Learning from the Most Popular Customer-Centric Company

Amazon is still growing rapidly due to its focus on the customer. There are a few areas where Amazon teaches business owners how to become customer-centric.

Improving Customer Experience

One way Jeff Bezos has made Amazon the "go-to" site for online shoppers is by looking for innovative ways to make customer experience much better. A few of these innovative ideas that have been implemented include the following:

- Providing product selections in real time using the buying

and browsing history of each customer to make this selection
- Offering the best deals to customers
- Making the ordering and delivering process fast and stress-free

Empowering Customers

The ability to help customers make purchasing decisions is one of the reasons why a lot of buyers keep visiting the website.

On the Amazon website, there is a feedback section on the product page. Users also have various options when separating the information on the page according to its relevance to their requirements.

The display of customer reviews is an idea that Amazon first implemented on its platform. Most companies also follow this model to offer transparency in the retail space. This decision by Amazon provided some consumer benefits, including the following:

- It provides in-depth knowledge of a particular product to significantly influence the buyers' purchase decisions. Previously, buyers had no background information on the product they were buying.
- With customers sharing knowledge, manufacturers now focus more on producing high-quality products to meet consumer demands.

Consumers are happier when they can make their purchasing

decision after assessing all the available information on a product. Your business should be able to provide all this information.

There will be critics who will have negative reviews to undermine your services and products. Dreading this idea is normal. Nonetheless, your customer will trust your business more if you are willing to be transparent. Although you will find many critics, you will also find a lot of supporters who will vouch for your product if they can get the satisfaction they desire.

Customer Loyalty

Helpfulness is the measure that Amazon uses in assessing the quality of its customer service.

The company provides easy surveys as a means to interact with its customers regularly. Some of the effects of these surveys are to create loyal customers and also to improve sales.

Although the surveys remain a vital tool, analytics is also critical in assessing the customer experience to ensure the success of the company.

As a company, creating and improving your relationships with customers is very important. At Amazon, this is achieved through their customer service.

When you make use of surveys, you can get in-depth knowledge on some of the basic ways your customers act, such as the following:

- What attracts them to your products?
- How do they learn about your products?
- Why do some customers stop buying your products?

Amazon suggests its surveys to customers through e-mails. As a business, you can come up with creative ways of suggesting a survey to your customers.

The content of your survey is going to be different from the survey of your competitors. It is because the information you need and areas where you need to improve will determine how you create a survey.

The Pillars of a Customer-Centric Business

Loyalty

You need to weigh the business decisions that you make over your customer loyalty. Customer loyalty is a priority when building a customer-centric business.

- Showing support to your customers will cause them to support your business.
- Offer a form of recognition and reward to your loyal customers.
- Employees who offer excellent customer services should receive recognition and reward.
- Appreciate your customers regularly.

Varieties of Products and Services

The actual needs of a customer should be put into consideration during the development of new services and products. What you think a customer needs might be different from what they actually need. In your quest for innovation, customer wants should be a priority.

- Be the first to offer products and services that the customers need. You need to watch the market closely.

- Separate your emotions from your business. Don't let pride get in the way of decision-making.

- Improve the services and products you offer through data and analytics.

Experience

One apparent pillar of a consumer-centric business is the customer experience. It is not your idea of the experience a customer needs. It is the actual experience of the customer. You need to treat customers with respect and empathy. It doesn't matter if they are right or wrong. To improve customer experience, you should apply the following:

- Treat both your customers and employees well. Treating your employees well will show how you want them to handle the customers.

- Your employees should have the power to decide on the most suitable option for a customer.

- Empathy is important. You need to decipher the customers' experience.

- It is necessary you meet the customers' requirement. It doesn't matter if you are on friendly terms.

Great Communication

Personalizing your communication is very important. When you have a large number of customers, you should make each customer feel significant. Don't make them just one of the numbers.

- Utilize a customer relationship management (CRM) strategy to manage your customer interactions and relationships
- Send e-mails that are relevant to a customer. Use customer types in creating segments for e-mail lists.
- Reach out to customers on important dates, such as anniversaries and birthdays.
- There should be a friendly, professional, and personal touch to employees responses to e-mails and while answering calls.

Promotions

Sale promotions are beneficial to attract customers. It is also vital that you think about your present customers as well.

- Present customers will likely recommend a new business if you provide ways for them to save money and keep them up-to-date with your price plan revisions.
- You need to honor any promotion that you are running. It can serve as a long-term investment.

Feedback

Feedback is an integral part of building a customer-centric business. Good or bad, feedback can help as insights when improving your services. Addressing the issues from the customer feedback can promote a positive review of the company.

- Keep improving on what you are doing right and correct the things you are getting wrong.
- Reviews and opinions are helpful in determining when you need to make changes.
- Your responsibility as the business owner is to implement changes. It is not the job of the employees.

Pricing

Your business should focus more on the value than the price. You must always offer great value on your products. It is not necessary for the business to always compete on price.

- Just because you offer excellent value doesn't mean you should increase your price as you see fit. Customers will remain loyal to your business until they get a better price.
- You need to look toward providing long-term satisfaction and overlook the short-term profits.
- Offering the best value matters more than giving the lowest prices.

How to Measure the Success of a Customer-Centric Company

Churn Rate

It is the percentage of revenue or percentage of customers that a business loses within a period.

Types of Churn Rate

User churn rate is the percentage of spending customers your business loses on a monthly basis.

User churn rate = number of customers who canceled in the last thirty days ÷ number of active paying customers thirty days ago × 100

Revenue churn rate is the percentage of revenue which your business is losing on a monthly basis.

Revenue churn rate = total MRR lost due to cancellations and downgrades in the last thirty days ÷ MRR thirty days ago × 100

Reasons for Churn

Churn in a business is often a result of two main factors:

- Cancellations
- Downgrades

Cancellation is merely a situation where customers stop their subscription. There are various reasons for this, including poor customer service, the discovery of a better substitute for your product, and a product that doesn't work as intended.

Downgrades, on the other hand, involve a customer opting for a lower product plan. It may be because there are no unique features in the more expensive plans.

Lifetime Value (CLV)

The customer is your most important asset when building a customer-centric business. The customer lifetime value (CLV) is the total profit that your business can generate while retaining a customer. It measures the profit that a company makes from each of its customers.

CHAPTER 4: Adopting a Good Name

A name for your business is crucial to its success. It is important in telling the story of your business. The name also serves as a motivation for what the business intends to achieve.

Giving your business a name is a rigorous process that takes time. You can expect the meaning behind the name to evolve over time. This is often due to experiences customers have with the business.

Choosing a name for your business can be difficult. With so many businesses available, getting a perfect name that is not taken by another business requires work.

Things to Avoid When Selecting a Business Name

Basic words don't stand out. When you are entering into a business category with a lot of competition, you need a name to make you stand out. It is also vital you avoid using names that are difficult to memorize. Names like Yahoo! and Amazon are quite catchy and easy to remember.

Don't name your business using words from a map. Adding the name of the region, state, or city where a company is set up is a mistake that a lot of new business owners make. Such businesses do not take time to look at the big picture. Although a lot of companies benefit from this method of naming during the initial phase, it affects their expansion later on.

There are lots of famous companies that made strategic changes to their business names to avoid limiting their growth. An example is Kentucky Fried Chicken. In addressing the issue that the name posed to its expansion into other states, it is now well known as KFC. Ensure you avoid this pitfall during the early stages of your business.

Do not involve too many people when deciding on a business name. There is an important reason why it is best to avoid involving too many individuals when coming up with a business name. The main issue with this method of selecting a name is the rift you will generate. Since you will be picking a single name in the end, you will need to turn down a lot of ideas.

Instead of taking this approach, you can limit the number of individuals to the leading players in the business. These are the few individuals who put the progress of the business as a priority. You need people who will set aside their ego to obtain the best results.

Obscurity can push customers away. The idea of having a business name is usually to tell a story. In a situation where this name is difficult to spell or pronounce or is too obscure, you may end up pushing away a lot of customers.

If you are thinking of using a Latin phrase, it is best you avoid it. There are also lots of fictitious names that may convey the essence of your business perfectly. But the problem is, how many people know about these fictitious names like you do? A lot of people will find such names to be a mystery in addition to being difficult to pronounce.

Understanding your customers can also be of help. If you are selling to professionals in a particular field, there are certain metaphors that they will easily understand.

Do not be stiff on a name change. When running a business, a lot of business owners find out that there is an issue with the business name. Regardless, they choose to leave the name as it is. It is a wrong step to take as there is no way to resolve this issue unless you take action.

We are all familiar with Amazon, but very few people are aware that this was not the original name of the company. During the initial stages, the company was Cadabra.com, but his trademark lawyer heard *Cadaver* instead. To prevent the same issue from coming up in the future, he decided to change the name to Amazon.

Importance of a Good Business Name

It becomes your motivation. Your business name should be able to inspire your belief. You have to believe in what the name implies. It is the only way you can strive toward success.

It informs your market. One significant importance of an

excellent business name is that it tells people what your business does. It is an apparent means through which your business success is affected by its name. Having a name that gives a clear idea about the business without causing any misunderstanding is priceless to your business. You can also explicitly define the character of your business using an abstract name.

It defines the business. There is a reason why you need to consider your future when selecting a business name. A name that doesn't set a boundary will provide room for the expansion of your business. Using a name that contains a geographical location or a particular service will prevent you from adding other services or moving to other areas.

It sets the scene for interactions. The scene for customer interaction is often set up by your business name. The name of the business often shapes the expectations of your customers. If the name shapes an expectation that doesn't align with reality, the customer is going to have a rethink. The business name serves as the first means of communication between you and the customer. A business name that sends wrong signals will cause your prospects to think that the business does not have a vision.

CHAPTER 5: Invest More on the Product

In the old world, you devote 30 percent of your time to building a great service and 70 percent of your time to shouting about it. In the new world, that inverts.

—Jeff Bezos, Amazon founder and CEO

Nowadays, people show more interest in what your product can offer. This is why you need to make sure it provides the best value. No customer will return if you provide inferior quality regardless of the price.

The taste, look, smell, sound, and feels are some of the factors that determine the quality of a product. Some of the things that make certain products stand out from the crowd include the shapes, colors, textures, features, and prints.

Details are significant to customers. These details can improve the sale of your products or lead to a decline in their popularity. The design of a product and the unique features that it offers has a considerable influence on the purchasing decision of a customer.

Simple additions, such as providing some color options, can make all the difference. If you can admit that the appearance of a product matters, then there are a lot of changes you can implement. One of such is to offer customizable options during the purchase of a product. Do you sell handbags? Can you add an adjustable shoulder strap to convert into a shoulder bag easily?

Why You Should Invest More in the Product

Maintaining Your Reputation

The reputation of your business is always on the line when you decide to sell your products. One significant factor that improves the reputation of your company is quality. It has always been common for individuals, both prospects and customers, to interact about the products that a business offers. Customer interaction has become more comfortable with social media. Social networking sites, forums, and product review sites have become popular destinations for prospects to get an idea of what a business has to offer. In a market that remains very competitive, quality can be the game changer for your business.

Offering poor quality products will lead to customer returns as well as return campaigns. These will not only negatively affect your reputation; it will also lead to bad publicity.

Controlling Your Costs

Producing poor-quality products will also have an impact on your business. Inferior-quality products are also what customers and businesses commonly refer to as defective products. It is common for companies to recall defective products from the market and also stop the production. In a case where a customer receives a defective product, the business will need to pay for the replacements and also refund customers for any returns.

Defective products do not comply with industry or customer standards. For this reason, the need may arise where you will need to pay off legal costs.

Compliance with Industry Standards

To comply with legislation, it is essential that your product undergoes an accreditation to a particular quality standard. Compliance with the health and safety standards is necessary for businesses that intend to sell products, such as electrical goods, food, or health-care products.

If your business can assure customers of accreditation, it becomes easier to get into new markets and also attract new customers.

It Becomes Easier to Meet Customer Expectations

A customer is only going to buy what you are selling if it is high quality. They can quickly look for another business to meet their requirements if you fail to deliver. The internet has made it easy to find and compare multiple companies offering similar services quickly. To retain your customers, it is essential you satisfy them. Providing quality products is the only way to satisfy your customers. The long-term profitability and revenue of your business depend on the quality of the products you offer. Once you can assure users of quality, it becomes a lot easier to get customers to purchase your products even when the prices may be higher than competitors.

How Does It Improve Your Business?

It promotes recommendations and word of mouth. When deciding on a purchase, a large percentage of individuals are more likely to follow the advice of a family member or friend. This is why word of mouth remains a great way to influence a consumer.

Online and offline, word of mouth remains a very influential factor in purchase-related decisions. Customers want to know if there is anyone who has made use of the product. What was their experience with such a product? This is where the input of family and friends come in. Forums and review sites also help in promoting a product through word of mouth.

For a company that offers products with high quality, it is much easier to get recommendations and positive reviews from customers.

It minimizes returns and complaints from customers. To ensure that there is a low rate of returns and fewer complaints from customers, it is crucial that your business invests more money and time on each product. With such a high-quality product, your company will also enjoy repeat purchase.

As a new business, you can expect to spend more when

convincing customers to try your new products. It is usually because the price of high-quality products is often quite high for new-entry products. If your business can satisfy a customer during the initial use of a product, the chances that these same individuals will return to make another purchase is very high.

What can you do as a business titan? If you are looking for honest and blunt opinions, then you should consider a market research group. You can also offer the product to potential customers to test it for free. The opinions that you get will help you understand the areas where you can improve on the product.

Do not assume that you can release a product of the best quality without getting an opinion from the market. It is common to get the best feedback from the eyes of an amateur.

You enjoy a higher return on investments. It is easy to note that with high-quality products, the return on investment (ROI) is much higher. According to studies, there is a solid relationship between profitability and quality.

If your product has lower field failures and defects, the costs of service and manufacturing will also be more economical. It is only applicable if the cost of defect prevention remains lower than the profits.

What can you do as a business titan? After producing a high-quality product and completing the marketing of the product, the next step is to look for areas where you can reduce the cost of production. Any area where you choose to reduce this cost must not lead to a compromise in the quality of your product.

CHAPTER 6: Sell Premium Products at Nonpremium Prices

There are two kinds of companies, those that work to try to charge more and those that work to charge less. We will be the second.

—*Jeff Bezos, Amazon founder and CEO*

If you take a quick assessment of online shoppers, you notice that the first website they visit is Amazon. Why? There is a general assumption that products on this e-commerce website are much cheaper than what is available on any other site.

The truth is that not all products on Amazon are cheaper than what you find elsewhere. Amazon implements a trick to get users to think their prices are more affordable.

How Does Amazon Pricing Influence Consumer Thinking?

When you shop on Amazon, there are certain products that are very popular. These are also known as premium products. Amazon focuses on these particular products and places a significant amount of discount on such products. After setting the discount on these products, they are a lot cheaper than what you find on the website of any competitor. As a result of the popularity of these products, individuals looking to make a purchase will find their way to the Amazon website.

As individuals can get these great deals more often, they begin to assume that Amazon is the best site for shopping for items at a great price. Since a lot of customers are confident in the services of Amazon, they may overlook the need to compare prices on other sites.

This is where things get a lot better for Amazon. Since the prices on premium products are at nonpremium prices, what about the nonpremium products? If you decide to shop for other accessories, such as a webcam, keyboard, HDMI cable, or router to complement the sweet deal you got on a 4K TV or a laptop, you may end up paying an additional 25 percent or more on the actual price of these accessories.

In essence, it merely means that while the price of the most popular laptop on Amazon may be the cheapest you can find, the second most popular laptop may be the more expensive than what you get elsewhere.

CHAPTER 7: Build a Culture

Cultures aren't so much planned as they evolve from that early set of people.

—*Jeff Bezos, Amazon founder and CEO*

If you are running a business, your workers should not be afraid of going to the workplace on any day. They have to love being at their job. The atmosphere, new challenges, and interaction with colleagues should make them want to stay.

It is understandable that a job may sometimes pose difficulties, but there shouldn't be additional stress due to the culture. The importance of workplace culture is to help ease stress that an employee experiences due to work.

Culture is essential to sustain the enthusiasm of your employees. The productivity of a company depends on the happiness of the employees. By improving the productivity of your business, you can outperform your competitors.

It becomes easier to implement principles that guide your business when you have a culture. Having a unique culture is also a great way to attract talent to your business.

Elements of a Business Culture?

Hires Who Are Excellent Fits

Individuals you hire to work in your business environment also serve as a representative of your business when they are outside the workplace. Depending on how your employee behaves to an individual outside the workplace will give a general impression of the inner workings of the business.

It is effortless to change your perception of a business if you interact with one of its employees. If the employee is generally nice, you have a positive perception. On the other hand, an employee who behaves rudely will paint a negative picture of the company.

The impact of employee interaction can be much more significant if you are hearing about the company for the first time. Since this is the first impression you will be getting, it holds a lot more value. It makes it an essential task to hire individuals who share the values of your business.

Hiring an individual who doesn't share your values can have a negative impact on your customers and your workers. Word will get around that there is a bad hire, and it will be the topic of discussion within the organization.

The good news is that you can reverse the effect of this bad hire if you take the right action. Dismissing this bad hire will reaffirm the business values. It shows your employees how serious you are about maintaining the culture within the workplace.

Employees Who Understand the Business Values and the Mission

There is a reason why some individuals get a job from a particular business where a lot of others fail. In most cases, their success has a lot to do with their answer to a specific interview question: "Why do you want to work here?"

An interviewee's answer to this question can give the interviewer a general idea of how much effort has been put into research. Nonetheless, the only sure way to find out if an employee adopts the mission and values of your business is to watch them work.

Are your values a part of their daily life, or do they merely tell you what you want to hear for the duration of the interview?

If your employees adopt the mission and values of the business, they will do everything in their power to complete this mission. As a result, they are continuously promoting the success of the business.

Anyone Can Inspire a Great Decision

The fastest way to lose talent to other businesses is to limit the decision-making process of your business to the management. As a business gets bigger, limitations in employee freedom take effect. It is common to alienate employees from the decision-making processes, and this can have a massive impact on the work environment.

All you achieve in such situation is creating a culture where employees come to work, wait for the next order, and do what is required of them. This is how you create mediocre employees—employees who cannot think of better ways to perform a task.

The top-tier employees want to challenge themselves. They want to make a positive impact. They know that there is no need for approval from the management when creating a design that will improve productivity. They understand that the superiors are not always right.

When you hire employees who possess talent and also adopt the business culture, eliminating hierarchy in business usually results in success. It also becomes easier to pull talent toward your company.

Define Your Employees as Your Team

Defining yourself as a group of individuals is not the same as being a team. The problem with a group of individuals is that everyone is of the view that he is separate from the other. Individuals are more familiar with either having a part in a bigger project or working on a project on their own. Putting these individuals together, you have a group of people who are forcing themselves to work with one another.

As a team, there is a bond that keeps everyone working together. Getting credit for a project is not the primary goal.

The idea is to help each other out with the primary purpose of completing a project.

In sports, like football and basketball, it is easy to understand the importance of working as a team. Although there are situations where a single player may go on offense and beat the opposing team, it is not sustainable. There will be the need to involve other members of the team to win the game. Players who decide to ignore teamwork receive smaller playing time as punishment.

How to Create a Business Culture

Outline What the Values and Culture of the Business Should Be

There are specific questions that you need to answer when developing a business culture. These include the following:

- What is the reason for our existence?
- What vision do we have for the company?
- What values are important to use?

These questions are basic questions. Nonetheless, you will need to have answers to these basic questions so that your employees can know where they are heading. It also helps you see if you are all aligned.

Once you determine the company culture, make sure that you and your employees can live by these values. Let every interaction with customers leave an experience befitting of the business values.

Is Your Culture Okay as It Is?

A business culture starts developing from the first person in the company. The initial business culture will revolve around the circumstances of this individual. As employees increase, you can identify the business culture in existence.

The board culture also has a significant impact on the business culture in the early stages. You have to ensure you are making an investment in the board culture as well as the business culture.

A People Person Is Important in Building a Business Culture

The operation of the business culturally is also influenced by the right people with suitable backgrounds and personalities. Hiring a people person at this stage has a significant impact. A people person is an individual with experience on how to build a culture.

Such an individual should have been in a company with excellent business culture. It is not the same as an HR professional. Another mistake you should avoid is to depend solely on your people person for building your culture. It is the duty of everyone.

When building up from a small business, don't try to host too many social events. Unlike larger companies, your employees need their time to achieve their daily objectives. While you may be aiming for a culture that is socially engaging, you may also be reducing productivity.

Emphasize the Values of the Business Regularly

For your business culture to thrive, you need initiatives that will reinforce the values of your business culture.

In the case of Amazon, there is a Door Desk Award, which Jeff Bezos presents to employees who come up with cost-saving innovations. It is one way through which Amazon reinforces its cost-conscious culture.

What You Should Understand about Business Culture

Based on your business, developing a culture that is effective will vary. Each business will have a unique culture that will work for it.

The culture that Amazon is quite famous for is its frugality and high-paced work environment. Nonetheless, this approach is not for everyone. Jeff Bezos reiterates this point in a 2015 letter where he explains that this approach is solely for Amazon.

CHAPTER 8: The Importance of Frugal Thinking

I think frugality drives innovation, just like other constraints do. One of the only ways to get out of a tight box is to invent your way out.

—*Jeff Bezos, Amazon founder and CEO*

The common idea among a lot of entrepreneurs is that money solves all the problems of a business. It is far from the truth. Money only offers a temporary fix to most problems. Is your business not getting enough attention? Pay for adverts. Do you need to design a new logo? Hire an in-house designer. Do you want to impress your clients? Why don't you pay for a larger office?

This form of thinking limits the ability of your business to come up with creative solutions to a problem. Why hire an in-house designer for just a single logo? You can outsource to a freelancer. Instead of getting a larger office, why not impress your clients with high-quality services?

Looking at the way Jeff Bezos runs Amazon, we can learn about the importance of frugal thinking. Everyone knows that he emphasizes cost-conscious innovations. The Door Desk Award is a symbol of his frugal mindset. It reminds people of the early stages of Amazon.

What Is a Frugal Innovation?

A frugal innovation in business is a product or service that offers more value while reducing resources consumption.

According to Jeff Bezos, frugality encourages innovation. In a world where businesses are always competing, innovation is the only way to make your business stand out.

Attributes of Frugality in Innovation

It is important you understand that being frugal doesn't mean cutting costs. Through frugality, a business can provide high-quality products and services at a much cheaper rate. It is often due to resource constraints.

When your business decides to come up with a frugal innovation, there are specific key attributes that the innovation should possess.

Simplicity. By eliminating the complex nature of a product, it is possible to achieve a frugal innovation. It may be through changes in the design or how the product functions.

Quality. Just because you are looking for a way to consume fewer resources during the manufacturing process doesn't mean that you should reduce the quality of a product. It is the critical attribute of frugal innovation. It offers a quality that is similar to or higher than that of a regular product.

Affordability. In comparison to the regular products, a frugal innovation should offer considerable cost reductions. This cost reduction should always be from the perspective of the customer. As a result, frugal innovations have a cost of ownership and purchase price that is lower than other products.

Sustainability. Through the reduction in the number of resources a product uses, a frugal innovation can promote sustainability. It is important to note that some frugal innovations may be designed to meet the demands of a particular group instead. They aren't always an eco-friendly innovation.

What You Achieve by Thinking Frugally

A Better Handle on Your Spending

To enable your business to move forward, it is necessary you spend money. Regardless, ignorance can cause you to waste a lot of money. As a business owner, learning to control your spending can protect you from wasting money.

A useful example is in the area of advertising. Placing adverts in phone books used to be an effective marketing strategy at a point. Nowadays, there are few people who make use of phone books. So what would be a better way to advertise? The answer is online advertising. As a business titan, you are looking to think frugally and avoid throwing money down the drain.

Wise Investments

To create a successful business, you need to be able to make smart investments. The business needs investments to be able to get off the ground. Advertising, marketing, and equipment purchases are common ways of investing in your business.

When you think frugally, you can invest in things that are profitable for the business. As a new business start-up, you don't need to get the best office furniture just because you can afford it. You can go for high-quality furniture at a reasonable price. It can free up enough money to invest in high-quality promotional items that can attract customers.

Ability to Source for Funds

Business titans that thin frugally always get the best funding for the business. As a frugal thinker, you can source for bank loans that have low interest rates and opt to search for investors. These are funding methods that are cost-effective and safe.

If you don't develop a frugal mindset, you end up using funding methods that can put your business in debt early on.

Improved Accounting

A business owner who thinks frugally will understand the importance of excellent accounting. It becomes easier to assess the profit and loss of the business with improved accounting methods. Thinking frugally also makes it possible to save money by utilizing tax deductions effectively.

Ability to Take Advantage of Free Tools

Running a small business on limited funds will require you to use money effectively. To free up funds for where they are most needed, you can make use of free resources in certain aspects. You can improve team communication using websites like Slack and Basecamp.

Some Frugal Steps to Take to Improve Your Business

Outsourcing Jobs

Instead of paying for a full-time worker, you can outsource some of the jobs available. It is a lot cheaper since there is no commitment to send work regularly, and you don't have to pay salaries every month.

Advertising with Social Media

You can easily promote the services and products of your business using social media. Another benefit is that it is free. You don't need to pay for it; merely invest a bit of time. It can also be a means to improve customer interactions with your business.

Being slow on Expansion

Don't rush into expanding your business to other parts just because the money is coming in steadily. Having an expansion strategy is vital. It ensures that when you do decide to expand, there will be enough funds to support the move.

Networking with Professionals for Free

Learning to use apps like LinkedIn can connect you to a lot of professionals in the industry without costing you anything. You should also look out for local events where you can meet people to improve your business.

CHAPTER 9: Surround Yourself with the Right People

Life's too short to hang out with people who aren't resourceful.

—*Jeff Bezos, Amazon founder and CEO*

Every successful business depends on the team working behind the scenes. The members of a team come up with new ideas and strategies to promote the business. It is a reason why teamwork is essential.

Building a team of resourceful members is very important. Members who can think on their own are vital. If only one person does the thinking, the business is bound to fail.

How to Build a Strong Team

Hiring the Right Talent

When developing your team, you need to recruit team members who are the right fit. All members of the team should have a passion for the job and the business to ensure its success.

As a business titan, you are looking to hire talents with different strengths, background, and perspectives. These individuals should also have the necessary experience and skill to make them suitable for the job. The interview of a prospective employee plays a vital role in assessing if they are a good fit for the business.

Since this is the first step in building the right team, you need to have goals. These goals can be to hire a talent who is committed, collaborative, and competent.

Diversity Is Important

For the success of a business, there should be diversity in your team. When I talk about diversity, this refers to different educational backgrounds, culture, race, gender, and more.

Diversity opens the doors to new ideas with people offering different perspectives in solving the same problem. Knowing the struggles of a particular demographic will make it easier to provide solutions to their problems.

Just because you hire individuals with talent doesn't imply that they are excellent in all areas. Each person has unique strengths and weaknesses. For this reason, your team should consist of members who complement one another.

It will also be useful when making decisions. There will be a need to create a strategy using ideas from every individual. A single person making all the decisions is a recipe for failure.

Set Goals for the Team

To build a great team, you have to make everyone understand what they are working toward. These goals must align with the vision and mission of the business to be effective. There should be input from each team member when developing team goals. It is an essential step in letting everyone know their value on the team.

Effective Communication

Lack of proper communication channels can make team members seem alienated. There is nothing worse than finding out there is a piece of information that everyone has but you didn't receive. Transparency is critical when building a team.

Workflow of a team is more productive with an open channel of communication. An app that is gaining more traction in work environments is Slack. This app makes it easier for team members to communicate with one another and share ideas.

The Importance of a Great Team Leader

Nowadays, teams in a business environment often include individuals from different generations. It is because the workforce now contains individuals between the age of eighteen and seventy years. Common problems that these teams face are lack of effective collaboration and communication.

When selecting a team leader, it should be a person who understands generational differences. It is also important to note that there is a unique strength that each generation can bring to a team. A team leader should be able to harness the unique strengths of each generation for the right results.

Tweaking Your Hiring Process to Bring in the Right Individuals

The people you hire during the early stages of the business will have a considerable influence on your business culture. During the assessment of a new hire, it is essential you consider the cultural aspect in addition to the skill. Most new businesses make the mistake of choosing new hires based on talent alone.

Some steps you can take to ensure you are making the right choice when picking a new hire include the following:

- **Assess the culture and values of the candidate**: To ensure that everyone is following the same direction, the values and culture of your business should align with the new hire.

- **Use more than one interviewer**: To improve your hiring process, you need to split each area of the assessment and assign it to various individuals. It makes it possible for each interviewer to assess a specific area within the time frame accurately.

- **Place a priority on attitude**: Finding a candidate with the right skill and experience is often very attractive to a small business. You don't need to waste time and money on training. One common issue with such hires is that they usually have to leave the company once the immediate need for their services no longer exists.

- **Diversity is essential:** Avoid hiring individuals who all think alike or similar to you. It is crucial you can get varying opinions. Each new hire should be able to add something new. It can be background, experience, ideas, etc.

CHAPTER 10: Long-Term Thinking

There is a reason why long-term thinking is an essential part of a business titan. It doesn't matter if you open the right business or build a customer-centric business. Without the ability to think long-term, you will give up early.

You need to be able to accept a lot of things as part of the process. It is similar to how you have to accept failure. Experimentation will not give you the right answer immediately; it requires patience and time.

Becoming the best in the industry will require you to come up with innovations and inventions. Perfecting an innovation will take a lot of time. Having a long-term strategy is also very important.

The English translation of the Blue Origin motto is an excellent pointer to the need for long-term thinking. "Step by Step, Ferociously." Blue Origin is a space exploration company that was founded by Jeff Bezos.

This motto implies that things take time to achieve. You have to take it step by step until you reach your ultimate goal.

What You Need to Implement Effective Long-Term Ideas

Patience. For your business to make a huge impact, it requires time. It can be up to ten years or more. During this period, you have to be patient. If you think patience is not important, take a look at some of the most successful financial investors. You have to believe in your vision of the future to be able to wait.

Perseverance. Long-term thinking will require a lot of perseverance. The road to success is riddled with lots of failures. It is easy to give up if you are weak-minded. Perseverance is an attribute that makes it possible to try again. It is through perseverance that you can learn from your past mistakes.

Discipline. Discipline defines your ability to create a strategy for your business and follow it daily. Through discipline, you can maintain consistency in your business operations over the years.

How Do You Implement Long-Term Thinking as a Business Titan?

Expand the Business

For the growth of your business and to become successful, expansion is necessary. An easy way to expand a business is to offer your product to new customers. It can be in a location where no one knows about your business or the products you offer.

As you put in the effort and successfully increase the reach of your business, your revenue will also increase. This will give room for the growth of the business.

Invest in New Ventures

Although Amazon is a very successful company, Jeff Bezos still invests in lots of other ventures. His other business investments include Blue Origin and the *Washington Post*. It is a rule every business titan must follow.

It is an activity that can pave a broader road to success for you and your business.

Offer the Total Package

To become successful in the long-term, you need to be able to create products. Depending on others for your business can be detrimental to your business growth. It can also mean offering a wide assortment of products.

During the initial stages of Amazon, it was merely an online bookstore. Today, it offers products that include home appliances, electronics, car accessories, and many more.

Conclusion

Your success as an entrepreneur depends mostly on your thinking. Learning about some of the principles that business titans follow can give you an edge. Studying and implementing the various principles in this book is the first step toward your success.

This book exposes some of the secrets of Jeff Bezos. It provides an insight into the steps he took to become a business titan. These are skills that you can learn and implement in running your business.

The first step to take toward your goal is to learn the art of risk-taking. It is a skill that will open your eyes to all the opportunities present. In your goal of becoming a business titan, this is a skill you need to harness.

There is no shortcut to success. Business titans are those who are willing to put in a lot of time and effort. You also need to understand the importance of a great team.

My final advice for you is to learn from your failures. On your road to success, you will fall a lot of times. Your ability to get up and continue the journey is what matters most.

BILL GATES

Introduction

Lauded as one of the wealthiest people on earth, Bill Gates, has often been admired by many due to his entrepreneurial skills. From a tender age, Gates showed his interest in programming and computers. By the time he turned 17, he partnered with his best friend, Paul Allen, designing a machine that would count traffic by making use of an Intel processor. Ultimately, the two childhood friends established Microsoft. With the successful journey that Microsoft has been through, Bill Gates has had profound experience in the world of business. Undeniably, he became one of the richest individuals on earth. From time to time, Gates would be listed as part of the Forbes list of the world's richest individuals; therefore, he is not only a renowned businessman, but he is also an example to emulate from.

Starting a business is not easy. As a matter of fact, most people have tried, but they end up failing. Interestingly, there are those entrepreneurs that fail, regardless of their good financial situations. There are times when Bill Gates would run bankrupt while running his first business. This shows that becoming successful in business does not necessarily mean that you should have money. This might sound awkward in the competitive business environment that we live in but, nonetheless, we are learning from the best. If Gates made it from zero to something, then it means that there is a secret to becoming successful in business.

Well, you are right. Successful entrepreneurs will have their own versions of the secrets that they utilized to become successful in business. The funny thing is that sometimes these secrets are the common things that we know of. Nevertheless, it still makes sense to take time and listen to what the experts have to say. After all, they say experience is the best teacher.

With this book, you will be informed about the rules of success that Bill Gates thinks are key to succeeding in any business. Also, this material will compare Gates' successful business tips to what other successful entrepreneurs have in mind. The main idea here is to try and find key similarities as to how one can be successful in business. An in-depth evaluation will also be done to determine whether there are important factors that entrepreneurs should bear in mind before starting, or while running their businesses. Besides, common challenges that lead to business failures would be closely looked at. Putting together all this information therefore guarantees that you are better placed to establish a business that could highly likely thrive.

CHAPTER 1: Learning the Art of Success in Business

Succeeding in business is something that does not happen overnight. There are numerous things that you ought to take into consideration for you to succeed. Interestingly, this is something that many have proven and tested; therefore, you should not be surprised by the similarity of advice that you get from different entrepreneurs out there. Ever since I began running my business, there are several pointers I have never forgotten to mention. These are the tips that I always offer to entrepreneurs who seek my guidance.

Passion must follow your way

Before you think of anything else, it is imperative that you take a step back and consider whether you love what you are doing. In business, it is not just about having sufficient capital to do business, as there are thousands of individuals out there that have failed terribly, simply because they have the notion that, with money, anything is possible. One fact that I am certain of is that passion must follow your way in business. *Do you love what you wish to do? Is this something that you have always dreamt of doing all your life?*

Having passion for what you are doing is what brings intensity. This infers that you will be committing 99% of your time, effort and money in ensuring that your business succeeds. Without the right passion, there is a likelihood that you will only be working for the sake of getting profits. Passion will not only open your eyes to having a winning mentality, but it will also give your customers a reason to believe in your dream. With passion on your side, you can be rest assured that your customers will see themselves in you so, as you plan to begin your business, first ensure that you have the passion for it. Fall in love with want to do even before you think of doing it.

Hard work pays

Hard work pays, right? We have been told this over and over again. Expecting overnight success will only render you lazy. You will only be waiting for your business to thrive in 20 years or 30 years; however, with commitment and hard work, there is a certainty that you will succeed. Yes, other people might end up talking, saying that you succeeded overnight. Nonetheless, what they do not know is that you toiled and toiled over the years to get what you have now. Spend time with successful business entrepreneurs out there, and they will tell you how difficult things were at some point. It is never easy to get to your destination. There are numerous stopover points that you will have to make before getting to your goal.

A good example to emulate from is Bill Gates. He was not only passionate about his goal of running a successful business, but that he was also committed to it. Did you know that he opted out of college simply because he wanted to focus his attention on his dream? Ideally, this sounds crazy. Succeeding in this highly competitive world without a degree seems impossible, but Gates did it. He dropped out of college to begin his business. He dedicated 100% of his time in what he loved to do - programming. Eventually, the world is there to witness the fact that where there is passion and hard work, success follows.

Patience pays

If Bill Gates was not patient, we wouldn't be talking about him. He wouldn't have been recognized as one of the world's richest today. The journey to success in business is a long one. As such, it is important that you brace up for the challenge. Understanding that the journey is long gives you a reason to be patient for your business to blossom. We all know of the stories behind some businesses that started from nothing to becoming the world's admirable businesses; therefore, an entrepreneur should have the right mindset in knowing that the journey to success would be a long one, so they ought to be patient for their fruits to blossom.

Persistence

Besides being patient, you also have to be persistent. The mere fact that you are patient for your business to thrive does not mean that you should sit back and relax. Go over your goals and ensure that what you are doing is in line with your business goals. Embrace the idea of continuously learning and adjusting to changes around you. For instance, in the vast changing technological world today, it is important that you keep aligning your business to embrace what technology has to offer. It means that you have to adapt. Be persistent, but flexible.

There are instances where you might be tempted to give up, but persistence will remind you of the importance of running that business that you love. Early warning signs of failure might be indicators that your business needs some form of transition; therefore, do not give up just yet. Keep pushing to achieving your goal.

Walk with the right team

One of the secrets Bill Gates mentioned regarding having a successful business is that you have to find the right team. You have to find the right partner that will make sure that you are inclined to the business goals that you have in mind[1]. Right from the beginning of Gates' journey to success, he chose the right partner. Partnering with Paul Allen is something that he keeps talking about several times. Gates mentions evidently that one of the best decisions that he ever made was partnering with Allen[2]. Accordingly, initiating and running a successful business depends on the team that is walking in your direction. Find someone that complements your skills. This guarantees that they fill the void where you think that you are weak.

Think big

If you are going to run a successful business, it is important that you embrace the idea of thinking big; however, you should not rush into things. Thinking big does not necessarily mean that you should rush things here and there. Remember, as I had pointed out before, patience pays, so think big and act small. The little droplets that go into your bucket will eventually fill the bucket to the brim. The best thing about acting small is that you will always have a reason to enjoy the little success that comes your way as you run your business.

Make room for mistakes

Making mistakes is part of any business. The issue here is that if you fail to learn from these mistakes, that's where the real problem sets in. Make room for mistakes and ensure that you learn from them. The benefit that you gain here is that you improve. Your past errors help you to learn how to avoid such mistakes in the future. This is how you get to perfect things around your business. If you learn how to circumvent hurdles in your business, then be rest assured that you will be on the right track to succeeding.

Don't procrastinate

Numerous entrepreneurs will advise you that it is important to think about your overall business idea before making any moves. Well, in as much as this sounds like a brilliant idea, it is not. The problem with this strategy of starting your business is that it leads to procrastination. You will always feel like you need more time to adjust your business plans before you start your business.

Later on, you will realize that Bill Gates offers a bit of similar advice regarding the issue of procrastination. You should never procrastinate. If you are going to run a successful business, ensure that you do not end up developing habits where you postpone every move you want to make. Make risks. Give it your best shot and stick to your goals. This is how successful business people make it out there.

Learn from others

Running a successful organization demands that you humble yourself. Take time to learn from the best in the industry you wish to join. Invest your time in attending seminars and making notes on what you need to succeed in the industry. It pays to get informed on the ins and outs of the business that you plan to run. Keep in mind that your business might not be as unique as you think; hence, you need to learn from what others are doing. Perhaps this is the best way in which you will find an opportunity and take advantage of it but first, you have to do your homework. Research and learn from the best.

Run your business

There are many start-up businesses that fail because of management. When an entrepreneur chooses to run their business as though they are operating their banks, this opens doors to leakages. Mixing up your personal expenses with the business expenses, for example, will only lead to the mismanagement of funds. You will never get to evaluate how your business is performing. What's more, you might run the risks of lacking funds to operate. Take your business as a business. Monitor your income and expenses independently. It is the only way that you will know how best your business is performing.

Find reliable investors

New businesses at times end up failing just because you lack the right funds to run it successfully; nevertheless, it is wise to never give up when you know that finances might drag you out of the way. One tip that I always recommend to entrepreneurs out there is that it is good just to put themselves out there. You never know who might be listening. Accordingly, don't just give up. Present your idea to an investor that you think might be interested. This could be the beginning of your long journey to succeeding.

Again, Gates stands as a perfect example here. At the beginning of his journey to success, he, alongside Allen, presented their idea of MITS. MITS loved the idea and invested in what Gates and Allen had in mind. The point here is that it is never worth giving up on your dream just because you do not have the funds to operate it. Today, there are thousands of investors looking for ways of making the best out of their money. Be their target. You simply need to position yourself in the right way.

CHAPTER 2: 10 Commandments for Succeeding in Business

Succeeding in business requires that you learn the art of doing it. In fact, it demands that you adjust to the proven and tested ways of doing it. The path to succeeding in your business is a long one that is filled with all sorts of lessons. First, you have to learn about the kind of business that you wish to operate. You also have to invest your time and money in getting to know more about the industry that you want to compete in.

Additionally, it is imperative that you seek for financial support where possible. These are some of the considerations that you should put in mind before starting your business. I love to call these considerations - commandments. They are important, so, therefore, you have to abide by them for you to succeed.

Controlling your thoughts

Often, we have come across the phrase "Thoughts become things." Well, from my experience, this is true. What you think about is what you become. If you keep thinking negatively, be rest assured that negative things will come your way. The idea here is that you bear the power of controlling your thoughts. The last thing that your business needs is negativity. This does not mean that you will be dispelling negative thoughts from your mind. NO! In fact, there will be those times when you feel like giving up. This is a certainty. Your business will not run smoothly without ever stumbling. Nevertheless, it all depends on how best you control your thoughts so, rule number 1 is to learn how to control your thoughts to make sure that you always stay motivated.

The virtue of courage

So, you are thinking that your business idea is crazy, right? Well, are you willing to take the risk? Are you willing to invest your money is a business idea that you think might or might not work? Courage is what you need in becoming the best in what you do. Successful entrepreneurs will argue that at some point in their journeys they had to take risks here and there. Nothing comes easy. You need to be courageous to fight for your spot among the big players in the market. The important thing that you need to bear in mind is that you get stronger each time to overcome a certain business hurdle.

Follow your program

Organizing your time will lead you to the direction you want in your business. Running your business blindly is the last thing that you should do. For instance, make it your goal to open your store early in the morning, at the same time every day. Your customers will adjust to your schedule, and appreciate the fact that you are always on time. Customers detest being disappointed. Visiting your store each day only to find out that you are closed is something that would greatly disappoint them; therefore, it is recommended that you have a program that you can stick to. If this program means that you should open for 24 hours, so be it. Give your customers what you promise.

Find out where your happiness lies

There are times when I think the best way of understanding your customers is by putting yourself in their shoes. Ask yourself; "If I was a customer, what would I want in a certain product or service?" Doing this ensures that you develop some form of happiness in what you do. This is because it will be easy to find your way into the households of your consumers. To achieve this goal, you need to invest in some alone time. Take some time off your schedule and reflect on the business that you are running. Do you think that this business brings you happiness? Do you think that this business brings happiness to those that you serve? If your motivation comes from pleasing your customers, make it a priority. Focus your energy on this and be rest assured that everything will fall into place.

Money should not drive you

Most people would argue that money is evil. I tend to differ. Money only becomes evil when you allow it to be your motivation. If your motivation for starting and running a successful business is money, then it is wise to take another direction. Putting money as your driving factor will always open doors for you to get disappointed with ease. For example, if you fail to collect some amount of money, this implies that you will not be happy with the way things are running.

However, think of your business from another perspective. Find something other than money to motivate you. Perhaps you see yourself in your customers, and you wish to meet their demands. Their smiles could be your motivational factor. It could be that you need to see yourself grow in the business. Keeping yourself motivated without necessarily focusing on money is the key to thriving in any business.

Always find a way of adjusting

If you have ever sailed before then, you would know the importance of adjusting to incoming winds. A sailor will keep adjusting their boats to make sure that they sail in the right direction. This is the same thing that you should be doing in your business. Always adjust to industry trends that you know of. This could be changing technologies or new competitors in the market. Adjusting warrants that you are fit to compete with other players in the market. Rigidity will render you obsolete. If you fail to acknowledge the fact that your business needs change, you will run the risk of losing your customers to your rivals in the market.

Be a good loser

Losing is part of any business. Your losses today determine your future. How you lose today determines how you will succeed in the near future. You cannot expect that you will always be on the winning side when running any business; however, it is how you adjust to your failures that matters most. How well do you cope with a certain loss? Failing today doesn't mean that you should give up on your idea of running a profitable business. Certainly not! Learning from your mistakes guarantees that you are stronger to overcome similar challenges in the future; hence, it is wise to become a good loser in business. This entails learning from your mistakes and adjusting accordingly.

Keep going

Your urge to run a successful business will never be realized if you stop on the way. A good entrepreneur should keep forging forward. Distractions will always be along the way. As such, it is up to you to make certain that you are not swayed. There are those business people that would opt to switch businesses immediately they are told of a brilliant idea. While this might be a good thing to do, it is worth noting that you might be surrendering a million dollar business idea to your competitor. The only way that you will truly succeed in any business is by keeping distractions at bay and always moving forward. Yes, you will stumble here and there, but that should not prevent you from getting back up and continuing with your journey.

Don't expect miracles

There are those business people who would expect miracles to happen in their businesses simply because their rivals made it. Undeniably, we all might have come across the kind of investors that rush to invest in a particular business idea because it worked for other individuals. The last thing that you should do is to make such rushed decisions. Expecting miracles in your business will only ruin your entire plan. Have goals that you wish to achieve in your business. Set your mind to them and find a way of achieving them. In this case, you will have to put in hard work in meeting these goals. Your business expects you to be there during its growth to the maturity period. Nothing will happen by a miracle as every move requires your decision.

Find your obsession

Have you ever thought of something that you cannot get your mind off of? Well, whatever you feel that you love with all your strength could be the idea that you might have been looking for. Successful business people will go for their obsessions as a way of fulfilling their dreams. Some end up making money out of what they simply love. Your business demands this kind of passion. You have to find something that you are obsessed with and stick to it. The good thing about doing this is that you will never feel the pain of pushing yourself to the limit. This is the main reason why it is easy to succeed in doing what you love.

CHAPTER 3: Rules for Success from Bill Gates

From time to time, Bill Gates has been interviewed regarding the ideal ways in which he recommends entrepreneurs should stick to so that they can thrive in business. From his standpoint, there are certain recommended strategies that entrepreneurs should adopt to guarantee that they flourish in their businesses. Well, Gates must have numerous tactics that he has utilized to guarantee that his business thrives. Out of the many strategies, there are those that stand out from the rest. These rules for success from Gates will be discussed in detail in this section. Pay attention; it could be your wake-up call.

Have energy

Starting a new business is never easy according to what Bill Gates points out[3]. The worst thing is that there is a certainty that there would be numerous risks while doing business. This means that an entrepreneur should have enough energy that helps to ensure they can overcome that feeling of having to risk all that you have. Gates established Microsoft when he was only 20 years old. He was certain that his business would have to go through several risks as it was just starting up. Surprisingly, he was not concerned about whether his business would run bankrupt. His worry was about whether he could manage to pay all the employees[4]. To him, this was an issue as he considered the scenario whereby there would be some customers that might fail to pay in time.

It is true that having energy will make a huge difference to your new business. Think of this as having the right mentality to overcome any perceived challenges that your business might go through. This infers that if you think your business would face a financial challenge, have the energy to look past this challenge. Perhaps you are wondering whether your business would counter existing competition from big players in the market. The energy that flows in you should be able to overcome this challenge. This is what Gates recommends. Yes, you are sure that challenges will come your way, but your energy should look past them. Undeniably, this mentality will make a huge difference in the business that you are running, or in the one that you plan to initiate.

With regards to the above, it is important for an entrepreneur to expect that there would be different challenges coming their way; therefore, it is important that they have the energy to counter these challenges. But, how do you overcome challenges in your new business?

Collaboration

It could be that your business has several employees. If this is the case, then it goes without saying that your workers have got varying skills. They are unified together by the goals of your business; nonetheless, it doesn't mean that they have similar skills and knowledge. A large pool of employees should be an added advantage to the business as it could easily tap into the resourcefulness of the workers. When these workers come together, they could aid in solving problems with ease.

Keep in mind that two heads are better than one; thus, you can be sure that ideas from your employees will come from all directions. As such, collaboration is one of the ways in which you will find solutions to existing challenges in your business.

Be flexible

Flexibility is key when running any business. When obstacles arise in your business, you should be aware of the fact that there are varying approaches that you could turn to. This is to mean that one business approach could be better than the other in solving a particular problem. Similarly, a certain approach could be cheaper than the other if solving the problem requires some investment. It is imperative to mull over the wide array of opportunities that are at your disposal when dealing with challenges in your business.

Have a clear focus

Do you have a clear focus as to how you would be dealing with obstacles in your business? The worst could happen if everything is considered as a distraction in your organization. Overcoming challenges requires that you filter away all sorts of distractions that are not related to your business goals. With this, you will be focusing on the most important factors that guarantee your business thrives, both in the short-term and in the long run.

Communication

Communication is paramount for any business success. Interestingly, this is also one of the ways in which you could solve the challenges that your business is facing. Considering the fact that you are aiming to grow your business in the near future, it means that communication might be a challenge more so to remote offices. Nevertheless, it is important to ensure that you find ideal ways of making sure that communication within and outwith the organization is maintained. For example, you could opt to turn to the varying communication apps that will facilitate convenient communication. The good news is that most of these applications are free; hence, you do not incur any cost of using them.

Do what you do best

The challenge that you would face in your business could also be solved if you focused on doing what you do best. This is to mean that if you understand your product well, make sure that you polish it perfectly to suit your customers' needs. Maintaining your graph is perhaps one of the best ways in which you can assure your employees and your customers that you can overcome challenges.

Have a bad influence

This success tip from Gates sounds controversial, right? Well, it is. Bearing in mind that he dropped out of Harvard, you can certainly claim that indeed he is a bad influence. However, we are left with questions as to how he was a bad influence, yet he succeeded in business. One fact that could make this point clear is that after Gates dropped out of school, he convinced Steve Ballmer also to quit. Later on, when Gates resigned from Microsoft as the CEO, Ballmer replaced him so literally he is a bad influence – in a good way.

The main point is that when running a successful business, it is important to make sound decisions when you are needed the most. Gates dropped out of school to focus on his goal of running a thriving business. This was a game changer for him. He might have disappointed his parents, but he had a positive mind that everything would work out fine irrespective of the challenges that were coming his way. For that reason, your business requires that you make informed decisions when it matters most. Don't just do anything simply because you are the CEO. Pay attention to detail and be creative enough. This is what your business needs to stand out.

Work hard

Think about this; it only takes Bill Gates two weeks a year to take a complete rest from his schedule[5]. This is interesting. It shows you the extent to which Gates is busy trying to ensure that his business is on track. The difference between the business that you are running and the one that Gates established is; the strategy being used. It is true. The strategies of your businesses differ; however, everything else is just the same. Microsoft attends to the same customers that you also sell your products and services to. A thick line can, however, be drawn to the way in which you attend to your customers. In spite of the fact that Microsoft had become a big business, to Gates, it was never the right time to relax.

Most business start-ups begin on the right path and grow gradually. The worst thing that happens is that its owners get comfortable and relax. Without a doubt, this is nothing close to what Gates did. He attests to the fact that he only has seven days to relax and take a break from his busy schedule. This shows that regardless of the success that he has obtained so far, he still craves for more. He inspires many. Gates stands as a role model to most business people out there.

There are several ways in which you can remain consistent in pushing towards your goal irrespective of what you have achieved.

Focusing on what matters most

One of the main ways of ensuring that you remain consistent in running your business is by having a plan. Your plan should detail out for you some of the most important things that should be streamlined in your business. Similarly, your plan should also iron out for you the mundane issues that could be ignored or rather paid less attention to. Most managers that fail in businesses pay too much attention to things that do not help the business. Accordingly, it is worth having a plan that reveals to you the most important aspects of your business.

Set measurable goals

The worst thing that you can do to your business is to have unrealistic goals. For instance, if you plan to boost your gross sales by 100% in the following month, this will put a lot of pressure on your workers. Realistic goals should consider the resources that you have, including the number of workers you have, as well as the timeframe that you are working on. Also, your goals should take into consideration the fact that achieving small goals with time will make a huge difference by the time the year comes to an end; thus, admirable goals should be short. Set small goals that you can achieve within a few months. This prevents you from wandering and doing anything that might harm your business.

Communicating your goals effectively

Without a doubt, all your employees know that your business is there to succeed. They all know that you depend on profits to succeed in the market of operation; however, have you communicated to them about your specific goals? Do they know what you want to achieve in the coming two months or one year? If your workers are not aware of the direction that you are heading, then it makes no sense to guide them.

Running your business blindly is a waste of time and money. Your workers will never be motivated to aim higher. Moreover, they will never understand why you keep pushing them to the limit.

So, begin by effectively communicating your business goals to them. Make them understand why it is important to achieve these goals in your business. If possible, try to use some incentives to warrant that they do their best in helping your business succeed. Keep in mind that there are several ways of motivating your workers to strive for the best. This could be in the form of increased salaries or other forms of bonuses. Ensure that you know what your workers expect most from you to guarantee that you win them over.

Having the right team

Remaining consistent in your business also depends on the team that you have by your side. A good number of businesses out there end up failing because they hired the wrong people to work for them. This shows that the hiring process is of great importance to ensuring your business runs consistently and in accordance with the set goals. Your business consistency might be hindered by those employees that keep thinking negatively. As such, it is vital that you clear the clutter by finding positive-minded employees to replace them. All your employees should be accountable for their actions as they have a big influence on the direction that your business is headed.

Create the future

Does your business have a future? Where do you see yourself in the next ten years? Your future is something that ought to have crossed your mind right from the time you established your business. A business that doesn't have a future lacks direction. Bill Gates wanted to create a product that would be important, not only to his generation but also to generations to come. Coming to think of it, today, millions of people are using Microsoft. This means that Gates created a product that would less likely be obsolete in the market; therefore, think about the future that your business has. Mull over the products and services that you are offering. It should show you a clear path that you need to follow to ensure that your business could be useful to coming generations.

Have passion in what you do

Enjoying what you do in your business is the best way of tapping into your energy. What I do believe is that, when you have passion in what you do, everything else falls into place. You will never have the feeling as though you are being pushed around. Also, you will never have the feeling that you are being forced to do something that you don't want to do.

With regards to being passionate about what you do, the chances are that you must be wondering how you can tune yourself in this direction. Well, here are a few pointers to help you out:

Build on your strengths

Often, your friends might have pointed out to you that there are some key areas that you are talented in. This could range from soft skills to other technical skills, such as computer programming. Perhaps you are great at talking to people; build on this. It could be that you are good when it comes to analyzing people; make it your business. The idea here is that you need to identify what you do best. Where do your talents lie? What do you think you can do differently with passion? This is the main question that you ought to be asking yourself. Ensure that you capitalize on what you think you can do best to ensure that it becomes a business developed from your passion.

Have a vision

It is not surprising to learn that most people would argue that the amount of money and time limits the vision that they have; however, it is worth pointing out that your vision should not be limited by these factors. Having such a vision only limits you from reaching your potential so, what should you do? Begin by looking at your business from a perspective where there are no money or time obstacles. This will open your eyes to the realization that you can achieve anything only if you commit yourself to it. The main question that you should ask yourself is; "What if these obstacles were not present? What would I do differently?"

Think twice before you leap

Let's be honest with each other; there are times when it takes more than just your passion to run a booming business. Before making any rushed decisions, it is worth taking time to know what other people have to say concerning the business that you wish to run. Find time to reach out to investors who are already making it in the business field that you wish to invest in. They should give you some information on the do's and don'ts of such businesses. Once you have all the necessary information, and still you find that you are passionate about the task, take up the challenge. The main issue is to make sure that you are making the right decision as your business will demand a lot from you.

Focus on a larger purpose

Individuals like Bill Gates will always stand out from the crowd because of the large vision that they have. These people do not have a limited perspective towards running their businesses. They are always thinking about the bigger picture. For example, Gates is always thinking about solving some of the world's biggest problems. This means that the bar is always raised for him. Having such kind of mentality warrants that you are not stuck in your comfort zone. Perhaps this helps us understand why Gates is always committed to his business regardless of the achievement that he has made so far.

Ask

Running a successful business is a daunting task for sure. There are times when one could easily get overexcited about the way their business is running. What's more, you could also be overexcited about the idea that you have just thought about. Does this mean that you should begin the business right away? No! First, take your time to ask for advice where possible. We are human beings, and thus there is no guarantee that you will be making the right decisions now and then. For that reason, it is imperative that you consider asking for tips here and there.

According to Bill Gates, asking for advice does not necessarily mean that you should rely on experts alone[6]. Ask for help from friends and relatives. Seek their assistance whenever you feel that your judgment might not be reasonable. Arguably, they will give you tips here and there on the best decision that you can take.

There are several reasons why it is important to ask for advice as you run your business.

Gaining varying insights

Different people have got a different way of thinking. The mere fact that you are asking for help does not mean that you are weak. Get that right. Asking for help implies that you will be opening yourself to other brilliant versions of your idea. As such, it won't break a bone if you took time to ask for help from those that are around you.

You get to protect your most valuable asset

As a wise entrepreneur, you ought to understand that when you get to the position of asking for help, this means that you are at your breaking point. If you end up taking in too much, then you risk losing it. You could lose everything if you make the wrong decision from this point. To be on the safe side, simply ask. Don't hesitate to ask for help whenever you feel stuck. Besides, as pointed out above, asking for help doesn't imply that you are weak. On the contrary, it makes you stronger and less vulnerable to the challenges that are on your way.

Harnessing the power of gratitude

We all know how it feels when we help someone, right? Indeed, there is a good feeling that comes with it. When you help someone, you garner the feeling that you have helped the entire world to achieve something that they once saw impossible. This means that when you ask for help from people around you, you bless them with this power. In other words, you make them feel good about themselves. For instance, if you took time to ask your trusted employees on what they think is best for your business, you give them a good feeling that they are part of the business. They end up thinking that your business considers their ideas and, as a result, they work hard towards meeting your business goals. So, before you push away assistance from those around you, think about the power that is associated with such requests for help.

Choose the right people

In most interviews, Gates never forgets to mention that one of his best business decisions was deciding to partner with Paul Allen[7]. Choosing the right people to partner with will ultimately make the difference as to whether your business would succeed or not. Unquestionably, the shortcut to failing is choosing people that you are not compatible with. Before you choose someone to enter into business with, find a reason to trust them. Take time to consider whether these people share the same dream that you have in mind. Are they as committed as you are? The person that you choose to run a business with should be willing to go the extra mile and carry the burden of a new business with you. The worst could happen if you will be the sole individual taking on a larger baggage.

The fact that you are in business together means that you will also have to share the burden equally. Regardless of the shared vision that you might have, it is worth partnering with an individual that complements your skills. Choosing a partner that has the same skills like you will only open doors for competition within the business. Your partner might end up thinking that you are competing for the top spot in the company, so find someone that has different skills from you. This warrants that you work together in harmony over the long haul.

Embrace the idea of doing it now

If you think of a business idea, work on it now. Don't procrastinate. Do not wait to get the required amount of money so that you can set up the business that you are thinking of. Procrastination is a habit that will kill your business. This is because it opens doors for other ideas that might harm your business. Alternatively, it could give you a reason to think otherwise about the business. For instance, if you keep procrastinating to start a particular business, there is a possibility that you could end up inviting negative thoughts regarding this business, so it is best that you do it now. Whether you have the money or not, find ways of establishing your business as you move on. The first step is always important. You never know, there could be investors out there waiting for you to take the first step so that they can take it from there, so, just do it, make a move!

Don't moan about your mistakes

Accepting failure as part of any business success is one vital issue that will take you to the top. The mistakes that you have made along the way should not prevent you from achieving your dream. You have already made a mistake; learn from it and move on! Focusing on the mistakes that you have made in your business invites negativity to your side. You will keep thinking about the things that you have lost, rather than focusing on what you gained. One fact that you should realize is that, without those mistakes, you would never have formulated ways of circumventing them. As such, your mistakes are a stepping stone towards reaching your business goals.

Failing is equally important as succeeding. This is for the reasons that it takes back an entrepreneur to the drawing board. It gives them an opportunity to reflect on the strategies that they are using to run their businesses. If the strategies did not work the first time, it means that they need some tweaking. Ultimately, this is how one gets stronger and better in what they do.

Concentrating on your unhappy customers

Still, on the issue of learning, you should make it your priority to learn from customers that are unhappy about the products and services that you offer them. Taking time to listen to your customers implies that you get to understand them better. They are an asset to your business. Accordingly, they deserve to be listened to. Unhappy customers in your business will reveal to you the loopholes and weaknesses that your business is suffering from; therefore, it is never wise to just focus your attention on those customers that you think they make your business profitable. After carefully listening to them, ensure that you take desirable actions that will see to it that their demands are upheld. Such changes are what your business needs to flourish in the long run.

Persistence and determination

From the journey that Bill Gates has been through, we cannot deny the fact that there are no shortcuts to succeeding in business. Persistence is what is required to ensure that you get to your destination. One fact that was pointed out earlier on is that you should always remember that the journey to success in business is a long road. To most successful entrepreneurs, they would argue that there is no point where you feel satisfied.

Well, this doesn't mean that they are greedy; it means that they are persistent on their goal. It shows us that getting money is not the overall goals that should drive our businesses. If this was the goal that drove Gates to establish Microsoft, then he should be somewhere on a vacation, but it's not. He understands perfectly that it is more than just money. It is all about making this world a better place to live in.

CHAPTER 4: Critical Factors that Determine the Success of a Business

Besides taking your time to learn from the best, there are certain independent factors that will have an impact on whether your business will thrive or not. Capital, for example, will have an impact on the direction that your business will take from the word go. We live in an environment where investors only invest in business ideas that sound lucrative; therefore, if your business idea does not sound profitable, there is a good chance that investors might think of something else so, without capital, you will be paralyzed. Unfortunately, we also have a few philanthropists that can help you out. This means that it is up to you to find the right business idea that will attract the investor's attention. Far from capital, there are other factors that you should bear in mind as they determine the success or failure of your business. Some of these factors are briefly looked at in the following lines:

The business idea

People start businesses with different goals in mind. Some might launch businesses as a way of getting rich quickly. Others might opt to begin businesses as a way of diversifying their incomes. Depending on the goals that you have in mind, the business idea that you choose would vary. In line with this, it is recommended that you be careful with the idea that you wish to invest in. For instance, if you wish to get rich within a short period, then your business idea should also be fast. A slow business idea will get you to the same destination but slower, so it is essential that you take your time to determine whether your business idea will get you the results that you need. Simply stated, begin with the end in mind.

Timing is key

Successful business individuals will always remind you that timing is of great importance. They would want you to understand that there is a season for everything. Before you invest in any business idea, think about the season. Is it the right season to invest in that particular idea? For example, if you are thinking about establishing a resort, take time to mull over whether it is the right time for people to travel. Maybe you are spending your money to run a resort in a country that is affected by political conflicts. Undeniably, this will kill your business. You ought to realize that you might have the best plans out there, but if you execute them at the wrong time, they will never work, so timing is crucial for the success of your business. Keep that in mind!

Network

As you launch your business, or as you run your business, it gets to a point whereby you interact with other businesses. Business experts would identify these groups of people as a business network. Your business will not stand alone in the market of operation. There are other businesses that will work hand-in-hand with it since you offer complementary goods and services. Accordingly, having a good network with other businesses means a lot to your business. The most important thing that you should be focusing on is to strengthen the little connections that you have. This might call for meetings where you get to sit down and find ideal ways of doing business together effectively.

Customer loyalty

Part of the main reason for starting any business is to serve clients so, if your business cannot do this, then it implies that it is dead from the word go. The way in which you serve customers will determine the success or failure of your business. Also, serving your customers will have an impact on your growth. Ideal businesses that have made it to the top have a plan of serving their clients in the most enticing way. Organizations know how best to entice clients through the way they serve them. Your business will also depend heavily on the customer loyalty that you will be getting. If more customers end up being loyal to the brand that you offer them, be rest assured of success both in the short-term and in the long run.

Integrity

Which customer would want to depend on a business that does not acknowledge the importance of being honest and open? Customers are always in search of brands that they can fully depend on. Whether you are selling products, or simply offering services to your esteemed customers, you should be honest. When you fail to meet deadlines, make valid explanations. Clients expect that from you. Bear in mind that they are not getting the products and services for free. You owe them honesty and transparency. Don't expect your business to flourish if you cannot handle the demands of customers that only seek integrity in your organization.

Sales

If your idea is great and it lacks the right channel to sell it, it would create a huge problem. The way in which you sell your products and services will have an impact on your business. With the advancement in technology today, there is a wide array of options for you to turn to. For example, you could choose to invest in what people like most - social media. Sell your business through social media and expect positive changes. Social media is a great place to market your business since there are millions of people using it. This means that you will get a wider market reach.

Equally, marketing your product on social media guarantees that you spend less on marketing your business. Prosperous business people will point out that it is important to work smart, rather than working hard, so taking advantage of what technology has to offer could be your turning point in your business. Embrace the idea of taking opportunities before they are exploited in the highly competitive environment that we live in.

Build the right team

The ladder of success would be smoother if you hire the right people to work for you. No-one is rushing you to hire workers that are not qualified in your business. The benefit that you gain in hiring the right workers is that they will be innovative enough to foster your business to success. Besides, you need a reliable team that doesn't necessarily depend on you to make certain decisions. In this case, if you hire qualified workers, you can be assured that you will be doing less to guide them.

In line with the issue of building the right team, it is worth investing in personalizing the recruitment process. Design it in such a way that you will have the best pool of talent at your side. It is just like any football game. You have to bring together world-class players to guarantee that you become the best in what you do. In the event that you do not know how to go about the recruitment process, there are numerous consultancy companies that can do the job for you. Your priority should be to make sure that you bring in the right workforce to your business. This is a key determinant to the success of your business.

Final Thoughts (Conclusion)

Succeeding in business might sound like a daunting task, but if you think of it from another perspective, it is not. Successful entrepreneurs will agree with this fact. It is not difficult to succeed in business. Equally, it is also not easy to succeed. Those who have made it will point out that it only takes a specific formula to get to the top. For example, acknowledging the fact that you need to be passionate about what you do might sound impossible to many. Nevertheless, it is a well-proven fact that being passionate about what you do brings success to your side.

Having passion in the business that you plan to run offers you the benefit of doing something that you love. This infers that you will never feel the struggle of running the business. The motivation behind doing what you do would come from the fact that it would bring you happiness. Remember, having the winning mentality in business doesn't necessarily mean that it should be based on the money that you get. Bill Gates will tell you that running Microsoft was never about making profits; rather, it was about making this world a better place. His idea revolved around the fact that he could solve the problems that the world might be suffering from. As such, it is imperative to have the right mentality when running any business.

Similarly, hard work is of great importance to your business. As an aspiring entrepreneur, always bear in mind that nothing comes out of the blues. You have to work for the fruits that you anticipate. For example, if you want your business to become the market leader in the next ten years, you have to work for it. This might call for sleepless nights with minimal holidays. Begin with the end in mind, and you will have the energy to fight for your business.

It is also worth reminding you that challenges will always be part of any business. If your business doesn't have challenges, then the chances are that you are not running a good business. Having obstacles in your business should not prevent you from attaining your business goals. In fact, obstacles are a stepping stone towards achieving your goals. The main point here is to perceive your challenges positively. Think of them as a way of learning about the weaknesses that your business is suffering from. From what was recommended earlier on, learn from your mistakes and adjust accordingly.

While trying to learn from your mistakes, never overlook the power of unhappy customers. They are part of your business, so you should not ignore them simply because they are talking ill about your business. Unhappy customers are a good analysis tool as they help in understanding the areas that your business is suffering from. It is advisable to listen to these customers and respond to their feedback effectively. In the long run, winning them over will make a huge difference as you would be better placed to counter competition from rival firms.

It is also important to reflect on the relevance of choosing the right people to operate the business with you. Whom are you choosing to partner with? Do you trust them? Do they have similar ambitions that you have in mind? These are some of the questions that you should ask yourself before choosing any random individual to partner with. Bill Gates chose Paul Allen for a good reason. It is from his wise decision that he recalls to this day that it is worth taking time to invest or choose the right people to partner with. While working on this, ensure that you choose someone with complementary skills. Yes, choosing an expert with similar skills might sound beneficial, but think about the possibilities of conflicts of interest. You should be aware of the fact that there are times when you would disagree, so take time to choose someone you can argue with and still maintain the high level of a business relationship.

Most importantly, it is never a sign of weakness to ask for help whenever possible. Nothing should deter you from seeking assistance where you deem necessary. We are all human beings with weaknesses; hence, your weak areas could be complemented by another individual as they might be strong in those areas. Bill Gates requested assistance from friends and relatives. As part of learning from the best people that have made it in business, you should also embrace the idea of seeking assistance. One thing for sure is that you become wiser in doing so. Forget about the notion that you imagine yourself being considered as a laughing stock; rather, think of it as a way of standing out from the crowd by embracing the weaknesses that you suffer from.

Before taking any further steps in the business that you wish to establish, take time to mull over the overall idea. Is the idea worth it? Does the idea favor the reasons that you have in mind for starting that particular business? If the idea is not worth investing in, you still have time to adjust accordingly. The important thing is to get it right the first time. It saves you from the nightmare of making mistakes repeatedly.

All in all, it is clear that starting and running a successful business doesn't require magic. It only demands that you stick to doing what you do best. First, find your obsession and make it your business. It might sound crazy, but, in the end, you will smile and talk about it.

Good Luck!

WARREN BUFFETT

Introduction and a short Bio

Since 1970, Warren Buffett has been the chairman and the biggest shareholder of the company Berkshire Hathaway. He is referred to as the "Wizard," "Sage" or "Oracle" of Omaha by the worldwide media. He is famous for remaining firm on value investing and for the frugal life he leads despite his massive wealth. Business is in his blood. Buffett bought his first stocks when he was 11 and worked in the family grocery store in the town of Omaha.

Warren's father, Howard Buffett, had a modest brokerage firm and young Warren would spend days watching what the investors did and what they listened to. The man has grown into becoming an investment guru and one of the most respected and richest businessmen in the world.

Buffet was born on 30th August 1930 in Omaha, Nebraska. He demonstrated good business capabilities at a very young age. Buffett formed the company Buffett Partnership Ltd. in the year 1956 and by 1965, he had assumed control over Berkshire Hathaway. He was overseeing the growth of a massive conglomerate having holdings in insurance, media, food and beverages, and energy. He went on to become the richest man in the world and a celebrated philanthropist.

Buffett was married to his first wife Susan Thompson from

1952 until she died in 2004. However, the couple had separated in the 1970s. They had three children: Peter, Howard, and Susan. In the year 2006, Buffett married his companion Astrid Menks at the age of 76. In 2018, Buffett had a net worth of around $84 billion. According to USA Today, between the years 2006 and 2017 Buffett donated almost $28 billion in charity.

Berkshire Hathaway

Buffett used the various techniques he had learned from Graham, his mentor. He was able to identify undervalued companies and, as a result, became a millionaire. A company that Buffett valued a great deal was the textile company, Berkshire Hathaway. By 1965, he was in control of the organization.

Despite the great success of Buffett Partnership, he dissolved the firm in 1969 to focus more on the development of Berkshire Hathaway. He slowly closed the textile division of the company and instead, pushed the company into buying assets in insurance (GEICO), oil (Exxon) and media (The Washington Post). He was immensely successful in his endeavors and even the apparently poor investments in gold turned into a big success. The acquisition of the scandal-plagued company, Salomon Brother, was highly criticized in 1987.

After Berkshire Hathaway made a significant asset in Coca-Cola, Buffett became the director of the company from 1989 to 2006. In addition to that, he served as the director of Citigroup Global Market Holdings, The Gillette, and Graham Holdings Company.

Education and Early Days

At the age of 16, young Warren was admitted to the University of Pennsylvania for studying business. He studied there for two years and then moved to Nebraska to finish his education. He came out of the college at the age of 20 having collected nearly $10,000 with his childhood businesses. He received a Master's Degree in 1951 in Economics from the Columbia University where he studied under Benjamin Graham, the economist. He went on to further his education at the New York Institute of Finance.

He was greatly influenced by Graham's book "The Intelligent Investor" which came out in 1949, and as a result, sold the securities of Buffett-Falk & Company for three years. Then he went to work for Graham for two years as an analyst at the company Graham-Newman Corp.

Philanthropy and Recent Activities

In the year 2006, Buffett announced that he would be giving away his entire fortune for charity. He also committed 85% of his wealth to the Bill and Melinda Gates Foundation. The donation, at the time, was the largest act of charity given in the history of the United States. Bill Gates and Buffett announced in 2010 that they had created a campaign called

The Giving Pledge for recruiting more wealthy individuals for philanthropic reasons.

Buffett disclosed in 2012 that he has been diagnosed with prostate cancer. Subsequently, the radiation treatment began in July of the same year and he completed the treatment successfully in November. This health scare did not slow down the octogenarian who consistently ranks on the list of Forbes' annual world billionaire list. Buffett bought H. J. Heinz in February 2013 for $28 billion with a private equity group called 3G Capital. Other additions to the Berkshire Hathaway later included Kraft Foods Group and Duracell. Kraft later merged with Heinz in 2015 to create the 3rd largest food and Beverage Company in North America.

Drive2Vote was launched in 2016 by Buffett —a website aimed to encourage the people living in Nebraska to exercise their right to vote. It was also intended to assist voters in registering and driving the voters to polling locations in case they needed a ride. He was a vocal supporter of Hillary Clinton, the Democratic presidential nominee, and endorsed her in 2015. He challenged the Republican nominee Donald Trump to come and meet him to share the tax returns. Donald Trump did not agree to the offer, but his refusal in doing so did not affect the election results in 2016.

Buffett admitted in May 2017 that he has begun to sell the approximately 81 million shares he had in IBM. He said that he did not see the organization to be as good as it was six years ago. After another sell in the third quarter, his stakes in IBM dropped to around 37 million shares. On the other hand, he raised his investment in Apple by 3% and became the largest shareholder in Bank of America by exercising the warrants of 700 million shares. In the following year, he bought more Apple shares and made it the biggest common stock investment by Berkshire Hathaway.

The Venture into Healthcare

A joint press release was delivered in January 2018 by Berkshire Hathaway, JP Morgan Chase, and Amazon, in which certain plans were announced to team up and form a new healthcare organization for the company's employees. As per the release, the company — which is yet to be named — will be free from profit-making activities and constraints. It will try and find ways of cutting the costs and improving the overall process for patients with a focus on technology solutions.

Buffett said that the swelling costs of healthcare were like a hungry tapeworm on the economy. He further informed that by putting their collective resources behind the best talent in the country, they will in time check the rise of healthcare costs and, at the same time, improve patient satisfaction and treatment results. It was reported in March that HomeServices of America Inc. owned by Berkshire Hathaway — which is the second largest brokerage owner in America — was all set to take the top spot held by NRT LLC of Realogy. Buffett was hardly interested when Berkshire Hathaway originally acquired HomeServices. HomeServices was originally a part of MidAmerican Energy Holdings Co way back in 2000.

Early Life and Career

Warren's father Howard Buffett worked as a stockbroker and later served as a U.S. Congressman. Warren's mother, Leila Buffett, was a housewife. Warren was the second of the three children to Howard and Leila Buffett and the only boy. He demonstrated a knack for business and financial matters early in his life as confirmed by his friends and acquaintances. They say that the young man was a mathematical prodigy and could add large columns consisting of numbers without consulting business papers. This is a talent he demonstrated later in his upcoming years.

Buffett often visited his stockbroker father's offices as a child. He chalked in the stock prices on their blackboard in the office. At the age of 11, he made the first investment by purchasing three shares of Cities Service Preferred at $38 per share. This stock equity dropped to $37 quickly but Buffett held his nerve until the stocks reached $40. Then he sold the shares for a small profit. Later he regretted his decision as the Cities Service stock prices shot up later to $200 per share. He cited this experience as a lesson for having patience when investing.

When he was 13 years old, Warren was running some of his

own businesses such as selling his own version of horseracing tip sheet and working as a paperboy. The same year, he filed his first tax return claiming a deduction for his bike at $35. Buffet's father was elected to the House of Representatives in 1942, and his family moved to Virginia to be closer to the congressman's new post. At that time, Warren attended the Woodrow Wilson High School in Washington DC where he kept on devising new methods for making money. During his tenure in the high school, he purchased a pinball machine along with a friend for $25. Together they installed it in a barbershop. Within a few months, they made profits and bought more machines. Buffett had machines in three locations before he sold this business for $1200.

Career

Warren worked in his father's business Buffett-Falk & Co. from 1951-1954 as their investment consultant. He was appointed with a starting salary of $12,000 annually in the Benjamin Graham's partnership firm in 1954. His boss was difficult to work with and estimated strict devotion to conformist methods and investment rules. The young mind of Warren often questioned these rules but after Graham retired, he closed the partnership in 1956. Buffett had saved quite a bit of money by then. He used these savings to open Buffett Partnership Ltd., the investment partnership in Omaha. He began operating many other partnerships and by the end of the 50s, he had seven. As a result, he became a millionaire in 1962.

Then he merged all these partnerships into one and invested in Berkshire Hathaway. He purchased their shares aggressively during the 60s and eventually took over the company. In the latter part of the decade, he shifted the company's textile business. By 1985, the last three textile mills owned by Berkshire Hathaway had been sold. The 12 % stakes purchase in Salomon Inc. took place in 1987 and Berkshire Hathaway became their largest shareholder. Buffett was their director. But after a scandal in 1990, the company CEO left the company the following year. Warren took over as the chairman until the crisis passed.

It was in 1988 when Buffett began buying shares in Coca-Cola eventually buying 7% of the shares for $1.2 billion. It proved to be the best investment made by Berkshire Hathaway. Buffet entered a contract worth $11 billion to deliver US dollars against other currencies in the year 2002. He had made more than $2 billion by April 2006. It was in July 2006, when he announced that he will gradually give away 85% of his BH holdings to five charitable foundations.

In the year 2008, he became the richest man in the world with a net worth amounting to $62 billion according to Forbes. He surpassed Bill Gates who held the spot for 13 years in a row before that. However, Gates regained the spot next year overtaking Buffett.

Achievements and Awards

In the year 2011, President Barack Obama presented Buffett

with a Presidential Medal of Freedom. He is still the chairman and CEO of Berkshire Hathaway and is still ranked among the wealthiest people in the world. He is widely considered as the most successful investor of the 20th century. And he also is the biggest philanthropist of our time. He has pledged to donate most of his fortune to social causes.

CHAPTER 1: Famous Quotes by Warren Buffett

Here are some famous quotes by Buffett that could change the direction of your life. He is possibly the greatest stock market investor that ever entered the fray and has amassed a fortune of over $70 billion over a period of 50 years through long-term investments in stock markets. Despite all the riches, Buffett shows no extravagance and continues to live in the same old house he bought in 1957. His decision to donate most of his fortune to charity has inspired several billionaires to follow suit. Actually, he is known for his candid sense of humor and has delivered several quotes on investment principles and moneymaking. *These quotes are taken from various sources and will be referenced as footnotes and in the bibliography.*

Here are some,

"Honesty is a very expensive gift, don't expect it from cheap people."[8]

"Price is what you pay. Value is what you get."[9]

"Someone's sitting in the shade today because someone planted a tree a long time ago."[10]

"Be Fearful When Others Are Greedy and Greedy When Others Are

Fearful."[11]

"If you're in the luckiest one per cent of humanity, you owe it to the rest of humanity to think about the other 99 per cent."

"The most important thing to do if you find yourself in a hole is to stop digging."[12]

"Risk comes from not knowing what you're doing."[13]

"No matter how great the talent or efforts, some things just take time. You can't produce a baby in one month by getting nine women pregnant."[14]

"It takes 20 years to build a reputation and five minutes to ruin it. If you think about that you'll do things differently."[15]

"Rule No. 1: Never lose money. Rule No. 2: Never forget Rule No. 1."[16]

"It's better to hang out with people better than you. Pick out associates whose behavior is better than yours and you'll drift in that direction."[17]

"Should you find yourself in a chronically leaking boat, energy devoted to changing vessels is likely to be more productive than energy devoted to patching leaks."[18]

"The difference between successful people and really successful people is that really successful people say no to almost everything."[19]

"You never know who's swimming naked until the tide goes out."[20]

"I always knew I was going to be rich. I don't think I ever doubted it for a minute."[21]

"You only have to do a very few things right in your life so long as you don't do too many things wrong."[22]

"There seems to be some perverse human characteristic that likes to make easy things difficult."[23]

CHAPTER 2: Warren Buffett's Rules for Success

Buffett graduated from the University of Nebraska-Lincoln and got admitted to Columbia University after being rejected at Harvard. He completed a Master's in Science majoring in economics two years later and then attended the New York Institute of Finance. Since he was 7, he read about investments from the books he got from the Omaha public library. He is regarded as the Oracle of Omaha due to his sound business ethics and profitable investments. He was also ranked by Forbes as one of the 15 most powerful people in the world in 2016.

During his ongoing success story, he has provided a great deal of advice and here are his top rules for success:

1. Look for your passion

When he was asked about his staying power, Warren Buffett replied that people need to find their passion to be successful. He said he was very lucky to find it at the age of seven. At a very young age, he read a book called *"One Thousand Ways to Make $1000"* by F.C. Minaker, which he got from the public library. He mentioned that he was greatly inspired by it and began his entrepreneurial activities at the time. He advised students that they might not find their passion quickly, but they must take up a job they would do if they were already wealthy.

2. Hire well

Buffett, while addressing business owners, recommends three things when they are hiring: integrity, intelligence, and energy. He jokingly explained that in case the person you hired has no integrity, then you might as well have someone who is dumb and lazy instead of being energetic and smart.

3. Do not care too much about what others think

Buffett stated that it never bothers him when people don't agree with him. He is candid enough to admit that there are several things he does not understand and also that he tries to stay away from them. But there are other things that he understands well and he stays within his limits, which he calls his "circle of confidence." In case people tell him that he is wrong about something, he goes back and studies the facts. He is a firm believer in the fact that emotional stability is significant.

4. Read a lot

He has revealed that he likes to read. He reads five to six hours daily. He has also mentioned that he reads at least five newspapers daily along with a fair share of magazines, annual reports, and many more. He has admitted that he has always loved reading, especially biographies.

5. Keep a margin of safety

Buffett is considered the master of investments. He advises people to always keep a margin of safety. He explains in an analogy that a truck, which weighs 9900 pounds, should embark on a bridge with a capacity of 20,000 pounds rather than a bridge having a load capacity of 10,000 pounds.

6. Keep a competitive advantage

According to Buffett, the very nature of capitalism is that your competitors or other people will try to come and take advantage of your business by trying to take away your customers or market share. For you not to be taken advantage of, you need to keep going in the business and have a competitive advantage. One of the best methods of being competitive is by becoming a low-cost producer. Another method is to have better resources or possess more talent.

7. Have a schedule that fits your personality

Buffett has stated that he always has an unstructured workday. He does not enjoy meetings but reads quite a bit and is on the phone for only a moderate amount of time. His businesses have managers and they run by themselves, but his responsibility is getting the capital. He admits that he is fortunate enough to be doing what he really enjoys and be with people that he wants to work with. Buffett believes that having that kind of schedule is productive for him, as it fits his personality and aptitude.

8. Always be available for competition

Buffett says that if you look at the competition, most businesses die due to complacency. To keep a business alive, the owner must be a little restless to stay ahead. Therefore, people doing business must be moving all the time. Resting on the laurels is bad even for successful companies. Even when you are doing well, it is good to have the competitiveness similarly to when the business was just starting.

9. Have a model for success

Buffett was greatly inspired by a book written by Ben Graham. Even though he read other books related to investing, he was greatly influenced by the work of Graham. He sought after Graham and even offered to work for free for his company. He did work for Graham but with a salary. He even named his second son after Graham, Walter Graham Buffett.

10. Provide unconditional love

Buffett stated that his father gave him the greatest lesson he ever learned and that is the power of unconditional love. Buffett believed that it was one of the more powerful forces and a precious gift for a parent to give to their child. Buffett believes that any parent can provide this type of love for their kids and transform them into fine human beings.

11. Define your circle of confidence

Buffett has used the idea behind the circle of confidence over the years as a way of focusing investors on the operational areas. According to Buffett, what the investor needs is the capacity to evaluate the chosen businesses. There is no need to be an expert on everything that these companies make. You must evaluate a company from within your circle of competence. The circle size is not significant but knowing the boundaries is. All of us over the years have built knowledge in some sections of the world. We understand some and some require greater specialty to evaluate. Mistakes are often made when you stray away from discipline.

12. Don't Dwell on Mistakes

Even though Buffett is considered the greatest investor of all time, he has made mistakes in his career and is the first to admit it. These mistakes cost him billions of dollars over the years. He passed over some opportunities where he could have made billions of dollars, things he understood notwithstanding the things he didn't. You are only going to find out that you missed a great opportunity once it has passed so there is no need to dwell on a missed multi-bagger stock.

13. Surround Yourself with Great People

There are many great people Buffett surrounds himself with, starting with his first wife Susie. Their love story has also been covered widely. She passed away in 2004. She was a great supporter of Glide — an organization to which Warren auctions a lunch worth $2 million. Buffett regularly heaps a lot of praise for his Berkshire Hathaway team, and Buffett personally writes his shout-outs about people rather than CEOs who work on suggestions for them.

14. Don't sleepwalk through life

Wear your passions on your sleeve, he says. As he told his shareholders in 2010, there is nothing like following your passions. He loves what he does and has loved it all the time he did it. Some people are plain lucky to find their passions early and in case you haven't found it yet, you must keep looking. He also suggests looking for inspiration in this regard from the leaders of the sixty companies owned by Berkshire Hathaway. Especially focus on those that tap dance their way to the office each day, he says.

15. Paint what you want

Buffett can do pretty much anything he wants, but he wants to run Berkshire Hathaway. The reason is that he gets to paint his own painting. He goes there each day and works on three of them and feels like Michelangelo working on the Sistine Chapel. No one else may think that it is a great one, but he gets to do his own. There is no one there second-guessing him. He gets to do what he wants. And secondly, he likes applause. There are many investors of Berkshire Hathaway who have all their money in their stocks and are counting on him. When you can deliver for these people, that's the kind of fun he enjoys most.

16. Think independently

"People might think you are crazy at times, but you need to think independently to make up your mind," Buffett says. It is a responsibility everyone has. It doesn't mean that you cannot take inputs from others, but you cannot outsource your obligation to think rationally and deciding on the course of action. And ultimately, live with your decision. When you are convinced that your facts are correct, and reasoning is right, you should be willing to back your convictions with your money. It doesn't matter what everyone else thinks.

17. Be Rational

What prevents the horde of investors out there to invest like Warren Buffett? If sources close to Buffett are to be believed, it is his rationality. Charlie Munger is Buffett's longtime friend and vice-chairman of Berkshire Hathaway. He says Buffett's brain has a superb rational mechanism. Rationality is the single most significant trait necessary for investing successfully. The success of Buffett lies a great deal in his patience, discipline, and above all rationality. Rationalism is a belief that your actions should be based on knowledge and reason rather than emotional responses. Buffett doesn't get involved in the day-to-day vagaries of the stock market. He grows his net worth by buying high-quality low-turnover businesses.

18. Assign Yourself the Right Story

When Buffett was asked about his acquisition of the Washington Post and provided the analysis of how he judged to make the investment, he was asked how he did the analysis at the time and how differently would he do it now? Did he read all the material and how did he get his hands on all the material? And most importantly, how would he do it today? Buffett answered that he would pretty much do it the same way except that there are more opportunities these days. He met journalist Bob Woodward at the Washington Post back then when he had come up with a story about all the president's men. Suddenly, he became pretty wealthy. Buffett met him over lunch, and Woodward asked him: what do I do with all the money? Buffett replied that investing is like assigning yourself the right story. Imagine the editor asking the reporter what is the Washington Post worth? The reporter will go about interviewing brokers and newspaper brokers to try and value the assets. That is how Buffett will work. He will assign himself the right story. There are some stories he can write and some he can't. Then, he will go about investigating.

19. Bring out the best in other people

Buffett says it is a huge bonus if you bring out the best in other people. It is a rare talent, and it doesn't correlate with a person's IQ but with his attitude toward the world and other people. If you become aware of the talent early, it is a great asset. There is no need to be smarter than other people, but it will pay huge dividends.

20. Have Fun

Buffett says it is important to enjoy what you are doing. You don't need the IQ of 160 to be an investor. "You can give the 30 points away to someone and still be a good investor," he jokingly said. What you do need, however, is emotional stability. "If you want to beat Bobby Fisher at something, you will choose a game other than chess," he added.

Conclusion

Buffett has remained a successful leader for his profit-making organization for over 40 years. During this period, he has certainly become influential to many people but has remained humble despite his great wealth and success. He began The Giving Pledge and donated more than half of his wealth over the period of his life. He is inviting other billionaires to do the same. He has stated that he will leave his children just enough wealth so that they will feel free to do anything but not so much that they will feel like doing nothing. Warren Buffett's rules are worth considering for all successful professionals and are also useful in our daily lives.

CHAPTER 3: Other Success Rules of Warren Buffett

Warren Buffett is one of the most successful businessmen in the world, and here are some principles for you to utilize if you are doing long-term thinking:

1. Reinvest the profits

Once you have made money, you will be tempted to spend it. Don't. Rather reinvest these profits. Buffett learned this lesson early on. As indicated earlier, he bought a pinball machine when he was in school and placed it in a barbershop. He did not spend the money he made on anything else but reinvested it in buying more machines until they had a batch of eight machines in different shops across Omaha. When his friends sold this venture, Buffett utilized the proceeds to buy equity and start another small business.

2. Be game to be different

Do not base your decisions on what everyone says or does. When Buffett began dealing money in 1956 with an amount of $100,000 he had put together with a handful of investors, he was quickly labeled as the oddball. Another interesting thing is that he worked from Omaha not Wall Street in New York. But he refused to let his partners know where he was investing the money. Most people predicted that he would fail. However, when he closed the partnership 14 years later, it was worth $100 million.

3. Don't suck your thumb

Collect all the information you need in advance in order to decide. You can ask a friend or a relative to ensure that you are sticking to a deadline. Buffett prides himself on the fact that he can make up his mind quickly and acting on his decisions. He calls waiting unnecessarily and thinking as 'thumb sucking'.

4. Clearly spell out your deal before you start

The bargaining leverage is always at its peak before you begin a job. That is the time when you have something that the buyer wants. He learned this lesson the hard way when he was a kid. His grandfather hired him along with a friend to dig out their family store after a blizzard. The boys spent five hours shoveling, and they reached a condition where they could barely stand straight, and their hands froze. His grandfather gave the pair 90 cents to split between them.

5. Watch out for the small expenses

Buffett always invests in businesses that are run by managers who are obsessed with tiny costs. He said that once he acquired a company whose owner counted his sheets in rolls of toilet paper to check whether they were 500. He wanted to make sure that he was not being cheated, and he was right; he was being cheated. He also admired a businessman friend of his who painted just the single side of his office that faced the road.

6. Keep what you borrow within limits

Buffett never borrowed significant amounts for investing nor for a mortgage. He, over his time, has received many heart-rending letters from people who thought their borrowings were manageable but ended up being overwhelmed by debt. His advice to them was to negotiate with the creditors for paying what you can. After you are debt free, work on how to save more money that can be used for investing.

7. Always be persistent

If you have ingenuity and tenacity, you can win against the more established competitors. He acquired Nebraska Furniture Mart as he liked the way it was run by the founder Rose Blumkin in 1983. Rose was a Russian immigrant and built the mart from a pawnshop. She turned it into the largest furniture store in North America. She used the strategy of underselling to the big shots. Rose was a pitiless negotiator.

8. Always know when to stop

When he was a teenager, Buffett went to a racetrack. He bet on a horse but lost. To recover the funds, he bet on another horse and promptly lost again leaving him with pretty much nothing. He had squandered a week's earnings and he felt sick as a result, but he never repeated the mistake.

9. Assess the risk factor

The FBI accused Buffett's son and Howard's employer of price-fixing in 1995. Buffett counseled his son to assess the best and the worst-case scenarios that could develop if he left or stayed with the company. His son realized that the risks involved in staying outweighed the potential gains by a long way, and he decided to quit the next day.

10. Be aware of what success means

In spite of his immense wealth, Buffett doesn't measure success with dollars. As noted earlier, he pledged to give away most of his wealth to charity primarily to the Gates Foundation. He remains adamant about not funding the monuments in his name. So, there are no Warren Buffett halls or Warren Buffett buildings. Once you have reached his age he says" you will measure your success by how many people you wish loved you —actually love you." That, according to him, is the ultimate test of how you lived your life.

CHAPTER 4: Facts about Warren Buffett's Investment Lessons

Warren Buffett is a canny businessman, investor, and a role model for several people. His knowledge of investments and skills has secured him a number three spot on the Forbes World Billionaires list. His net worth is more than 70 Billion dollars, and he has reached cult status with amateur and professional investors following his moves. Media coverage is a part of the cult status. The Internet is full of stories about Buffett's life and investment decisions. With all this information, you can actually miss out on the interesting facts regarding the man behind a multi-billion-dollar conglomerate. Here are some interesting facts about Buffett and his investment decisions. We can learn a lot from them:

Fact 1: Buffett's biggest victory can be attributed to salad dressing

Allied Crude Vegetable Oil borrowed $175 million in 1963 from different lenders against their oil inventory. American Express was one of the lenders. And for the AXP, the loans turned out to be fraudulent. All the collateral was not oil but barrels filled with water and having a bit of floating oil on the top. The ACVO had just $6 million worth of oil and rest was all water. The ensuing scandal resulted in American Express losing millions and their stocks fell by 50%. Buffett took this opportunity to buy $13 million worth of their equity. Since then the shares have risen and have grown a great deal in value. It is one of the largest holdings of Berkshire Hathaway today. The lesson to be learned here is that always buy fundamentally sound shares if they are available at a discounted price. Do not just follow the market trends and take a contrarian approach.

Fact 2: Buffett's worst deal: Investing $443 million in Dexter Shoes Inc.

As per Buffett, the worst deal he ever made was investing in Dexter Shoes Inc. in 1993. The business soon lost its competitive edge when Buffett acquired the company. He says to invest only in companies that have the economic moat. Do enough research before embarking on investing in any business.

Fact 3: Buffett acquired Berkshire Hathaway for firing its CEO

Buffett bought the Berkshire Hathaway shares in 1962. It was a textile manufacturing company at the time. The textile business at the time was on a decline and the financial situation of the company was not looking good. Seabury Stanton, the company CEO, offered Buffett a verbal tender to buy their stock at $11.50 per share. Buffett agreed to the offer but was angry to find out that in the tender he received in writing, the price offered was 12.5 cents less than agreed upon. But rather than selling the shares, Buffett went on to buy more Hathaway shares. By doing this he became the majority stockholder in the company and then he fired Stanton. The lesson? Invest in organizations that have capable CEOs and manageable teams. Remember, in the finance industry all men are for themselves. By taking control of the financial situation, you will reap the highest rewards.

Fact 4: Buffett's first stock purchase was at the age of 11 in 1941

The first equity Buffett ever bought was from a small company called Cities Service. He bought six shares for his sister Doris and himself. After he had made the purchase, the price started declining and then rose again slightly to reach a value somewhat larger than what he had paid while buying them. He fell victim to the emotional pressure of market fluctuations and sold the shares. After he had sold them, the price rose from $40, at the time Buffett sold them, to $200 per share. You need a long-term vision for this. Long-term investments always need patience. Time is the most valuable asset for all investors; the sooner you invest, the better. Always invest long term as the markets will fluctuate, but the results will be better.

Fact 5: Most of Warren Buffett's wealth was created after he passed 50

On his 50th birthday, Warren Buffett was worth $300 million according to The Motley Fool. Today his net worth has exceeded $70 billion, which means he earned more than 70 billion after he was passed the age of 50. The lesson here is that the compounding interest is one of the secrets of investment success. Again, adopt a long-term plan.

Fact 6: Buffett, on average, made #37 million per day in the year 2013

In order to put this in perspective, take the example of Leonardo DiCaprio. He received an Oscar nomination for his role in the film "The Wolf of Wall Street" which was very popular in 2014. He earned $39 million for the entire year of 2014. Buffett made $13.5 billion, which is $37 million daily and $1.5 million per hour. Now you can fathom the man's wealth. Compare this with the income of the average American household in 2013, and you will realize the difference. All this is proof of value investing combined with the right temperament. It will always yield great financial success.

Fact 7: Warren Buffett holds relatively few stocks, but he tries to hold onto them forever

He follows a very simple rule of investing and that is investing only in industries and companies he understands well. And then he tries to hold onto them if possible. Berkshire Hathaway holds stocks of around 30 companies that include Wells Fargo, Coca-Cola, Proctor & Gamble, American Express, Walmart, and Johnson & Johnson. You must remember to invest only in companies you have knowledge of and then try and hold onto the shares forever.

Fact 8: Buffett spends almost 80% of his time reading

Both Buffett and his right-hand Charlie Munger agree that continuous reading and learning led to the success of Berkshire Hathaway. Buffett told "The Week" that he just sits in his office and reads all day. He justifies it by saying that his job is basically corralling more and more facts and info and sometimes checking whether that leads to any action.

Fact 9: His favorite meal is Cheeseburger with a coke

Buffett loves junk food and consumes 2500 calories daily. So, he is a true supporter and representative of the brands that he owns. He loves consuming cherry coke and placing a slice of cheese on his burger. But that wasn't the real reason for investing in Kraft and Coca-Cola. So, do not just invest in a company because you love their products. Buy equity in companies that have the economic moat, aligned fundamentals, growth potential, and those which are still trading below their intrinsic value.

Fact 10: Buffett is a big fan of the AMC crime drama series, Breaking Bad

Buffett created a twitter account in May 2013 and made his first tweet, which read: *"Warren is in the house."* He is also a big fan of Breaking Bad and the first photo he uploaded confirmed this fact.

Conclusion

There are many valuable lessons to be learned from the Oracle of Omaha especially regarding his approach to life and investing. You can see from these facts that his success can be attributed mainly to the attitude he has toward life. Buffett's history will tell you countless suggestions for managing your investments. You can improve your investing skills by learning from the past triumphs and mistakes of the investment guru.

CHAPTER 5: Value Investing Tips by Warren Buffett

There is no doubt that Warren Buffett is one of the most successful and natural value investors in the world, but he had to learn a lot during his time. There are many successful people who don't strictly follow the Buffett methodology and differ with him in certain sections such as diversification. But everyone has great respect for the man that made investing a lifetime pursuit. Buffett is a total value investor at heart, but he adds many insights in the shareholder's meetings and in the annual letters to them. So, it is quite simple to understand the Buffett investment philosophy. Here are some tips from the great investor that will help in developing a great and effective value investing strategy.

1. You have an opportunity when others are scared

Buffett once commented that an atmosphere of fear is an investor's best buddy. Those who make investments only when the experts are upbeat will end up paying a heavy price for reassurance that might turn out to be meaningless. There are many fears involved in investing like regret minimization, envious investing, and loss aversion. Buffett's reactions have always been unlike Wall Street. He will keep a calm head and avoid the fear, which always leads to over or under reaction.

This doesn't mean that you should throw the caution to the wind while investing, but fear is another animal altogether and leads to impetuous and many times, to incorrect decisions. Investing is an art of discernment without using emotions to make your decisions.

2. *Know your investments*

The value investing is not something that is left to chance, fate or luck. It is a measured approach to investments, and here you must research precisely before investing your money based on the understanding of the outcomes, which you have come to expect. So, know your investments. The investment decisions must be based on metrics that will aid you in calculating the potential and current value of the stock. These metrics can be acquired with the help of an in-depth study into the equity you are interested in. In case everyone is flocking the stock on Wall Street with great hopes of it skyrocketing, and are not sure why based on your research, then stay away from the stock. Always invest in what you know and can trust.

3. *Focus on long term results*

In case you find yourself in a tricky situation, you should guard your emotions better so that you will be in a position to walk away. However, you need to focus on long-term results. Value investing is about your insight into the growth of any business while constantly considering the risk, and it should be backed by data. None of the businesses grow overnight in value, at least the good ones don't, and the value investing asks you to stay with a stock for a reasonable period. Normally, most value investors will suggest a period of three years. However, it always depends on the stock. So, this tip suggests that you should not make decisions lightly, and you should stick with them until you have realized your goals.

4. Cash is King

Warren Buffet thinks that cash is a big deal. He keeps a lot of it at hand at all times. Reason? Buffett says that he keeps a lot of cash for withstanding any unprecedented losses and quickly seizing an opportunity for making a great investment. In the year 2011, in the letter to his shareholders, Buffett printed a note made by his grandfather in 1939. It said that he has known a lot of people who at some time or another suffered a lot in different ways just because they did not have enough cash at hand. He hopes that never happens to you. It is solid advice regarding personal finance. You must maintain emergency funds for any unexpected calamity or event. And you need to do the same with your brokerage account so that you can buy shares while they are dipping. For instance, in case you had some cash ready for investment when a financial crisis hit, you could have bought some great shares and sold it with 50% or 100% profits on the investment. But if you had everything tied up in investments, you would have suffered a setback.

5. Be cautious and fearful while others are being greedy

'Be fearful when others are greedy and be greedy when others are fearful,' is one of the most famous quotes by Warren Buffett. It is a great sentiment and very true for the stock market and the investing system. The bottom line is you need to avoid stocks everyone else is buying as most probably are overvalued. Rather look for equity which only a few people are paying attention to and check their fundamentals. Invest in these if they make sense.

6. Dividends are your friends:

Warren Buffett loves dividends like most value investors. They are great perks for buying a company as they generally indicate that the company finances are in good health as they are paying out the hard-earned money. He likes companies that have a long history of paying the dividends and even increasing them at times. There is a tracker available for these kinds of stocks, which list the companies that have increased the dividends over a period of 25 years. Buffett announced recently that there is a good chance that the total dividend paid due to his position in Coca-Cola will soon surpass the amount he paid for buying the beverage stocks. Now that is a great return for an investment.

7. Always look for undervalued stocks

Warren Buffett is a big-time value investor and tries to buy only those stocks that are undervalued based on their intrinsic value. He looks at the company fundamentals to calculate the intrinsic value for the last five years minimum and sometimes longer. He will look at the returns on stocks, operating margins, and whether the stocks have any or no debt. He will then compare the company with the peer group and see in case it is undervalued. Another key part to this is looking for companies that have a monopoly or special traits that empower it to be successful in the future. It could be technology or event management although Buffett has avoided the tech stocks in his time, as he doesn't understand technology. All these factors decide the intrinsic value of the company.

8. Buy and then hold

And lastly, Buffett is a true buy and hold investor. He always holds the stocks for a long period of time and continuously reiterates this to the followers. As a matter of fact, he has stated that he likes to buy them and keep them forever. This is true because he held onto many of his positions for more than 20 years, which is like eons in the world of investment. But he also says that this doesn't mean that you hold on even if the company fundamentals have changed. He will constantly keep looking at the company portfolio and if it loses its edge or superiority, he will sell or trim his position. Buffett is a firm believer in patience, and he basically doesn't trade, he invests. Look for the companies you like and then wait for a suitable price. It is believed that Buffett keeps a list of hundreds of companies that he would like to invest in, but he waits for the right price and opportunity. The last time he went on a purchasing spree was during the great recession when the stock prices were tanked. He was able to pick up deals and get prices that resulted in terrific returns in the following years.

CHAPTER 6: Warren Buffett's Investing Style

Warren Buffett is a great role model especially if you are looking to emulate a classical value investing style. During his legendary years as an investor, Buffett used to say that he is 85%, Benjamin Graham. Graham, as we know, is considered the godfather of value investing and was the first to introduce the concept of intrinsic value. It leans to the underlying value of the equity based on the future earning capacity of the company. Buffett, on the other hand, uses a more focused and qualitative approach than Graham. Graham used to find the undervalued and average companies and then diversified his holdings among them. On the other hand, Buffett favors high-quality businesses that come with reasonable valuation but have a capability for large growth.

Investing style of Warren Buffett

There are a few things to note about how Buffett interprets the value investing. It may surprise you. Like several other successful formulas, Warren Buffett's formula appears simple; however, it does not necessarily mean easy. To guide himself through the decisions, he uses 12 investing tenets or important considerations. They are categorized into various areas such as business, financial measures, management, and value. The Buffett tenets might appear cliché and easy to comprehend; however, they may turn out to be very tough to implement. For example, one of the tenets asks whether the management is truthful with the shareholders. It is not easy to answer that. On the other hand, there are examples of the reverse as well: things that appear difficult but are easy to execute. One such example is EVA (Economic Value Added). The full calculation made by EVA is difficult to comprehend, and the explanation offered by EVA is complex. However, once you have understood that EVA is a list of adjustments, it becomes fairly simple to calculate the EVA for a company.

The Buffett way is viewed as a conventional and core style investing, which is open for adoption. And one of the more compelling aspects of the method is its flexibility along with phenomenal success. If this Buffetology was to be a religion, it will be self-reflective and adaptive to the changing times rather than being dogmatic. The day traders require rigid discipline and adherence to formulas especially for controlling the emotions factor. However, it can definitely be argued that good investors must be willing to adopt the mental models to the current environment.

Business Tenets

Buffett insists on restricting himself to the circle of competence, meaning staying with the businesses he can analyze and understand. He considers the deep understanding of the operational business to be the prerequisite for a realistic forecast of the company's future performance. And he is right because if you cannot understand the business, how can you predict its future performance? A great example of this is when Buffett did not suffer a great deal when the technology bubble burst in the early 2000s, as he had not invested heavily in the tech stocks.

The business tenets used by Buffett support the goals of producing robust projections but first analyze the business and not the market, the economy or not even the investor sentiment. Next, he will look for the consistency in the operating history. Finally, he will use the data for ascertaining if the business has long-term chances.

Management Tenets

There are three management tenets used by Buffett for evaluating the management quality. It is perhaps the most difficult work for investors. He asks whether the management is rational. Is the management intelligent while reinvesting or retaining the earnings or just returning the profits to the shareholders as dividends? It is a profound query as most of the research suggests that management, as a group, tend to be greedy and retain the profits. This is because they are naturally inclined toward building empires and seek to scale instead of utilizing the cash flow that will increase the shareholder's value.

The second management tenet will examine management's transparency and honesty: does it admit its mistakes? And the third management tenet is: does the management resist the institutional imperatives? The tenet seeks managements that resist lust for activity and duplication of strategies used by competitors and their tactics. This last one is worth savoring, as it needs you to draw a line for many parameters. For instance, it aims to draw a line between blind copying of strategies used by competitors and outmaneuvering the companies that entered the market first.

Financial Measures tenets

Buffett has always focused more on ROE (Return on Equity) instead of earning per share. All the finance students will understand that ROE can get distorted by leverage and, as a result, is lower in significance to the ROC (Return on Capital) market. In this case, ROC is like the ROA (Return on Assets) or ROCE (Return on Capital Employed) where the numerator equates to the earning produced for the shareholders, and the denominator equals to the debt and equity contributions to the company. He understands this, but he analyses leverage separately thereby preferring the low-leverage companies and looks for higher profit margins. He also looks at the owner's earnings, which is the cash flow available to the shareholders and finally the "one-dollar premise" based on the market value of the dollar assigned to every dollar retained in the earnings.

Value Tenets

This is where he estimates the intrinsic value of the company. He will project the future owner's earnings and then discount back to the present. It is easy to do if you have applied his other tenets. He ignores the short-term volatility of the market and concentrates on the long-term earnings. He considers them only when he is looking for a deal. He also favors companies having a wide economic moat. It means the company has a clear advantage over the others and as a result, is protected against incursions from the competition.

CHAPTER 7: Why Warren Buffett should be your role model

Some people say that Buffett's net worth is close to $91 billion, which is staggering and enviable, even for people who are successful and unbelievably rich in a range of different careers. However, apart from his self-made bank account that began to grow humbly thanks to the small business as a child of pinball machines, Buffett has demonstrated several attributes that speak of his substance as a human being and clarify the fact that he is not just caricaturing such as Scrooge McDuck who just swims in the pool of gold bullion every day.

Some people might not be aware of the famous businessman Warren Buffett and might ask "Who is Warren Buffett?" but the way he went about his business and lived his life keeps on making him as relevant as ever before. Buffett was once asked how one should go about selecting a role model. He replied that normally because it's how they are: generous, kind, decent. These are the kinds of people you must try and emulate. Not shockingly, Buffett has all these qualities and serves as an example for those looking to be rich financially, spiritually and philanthropically. Elon Musk will need Mars. Kanye West will need Calabasas. Here are the reasons why you should need Warren Buffett the Oracle of Omaha:

Start Early

He began investing, as we know when he was eleven. He bought the shares of Cities Service for $38 per share. We are also aware that he sold the shares for a modest profit soon. But he was to refine his investing strategy totally, and then he understood that quick flips, although appearing to be a win, were not wise investments as picking companies that wanted to hold onto for long periods of time. His ethos of set it, buy it, and forget it comes from a notion that in case you had a chance to buy a good organization in your city and you knew that it was a good organization, knew that good people were running the show and you got it at a fair price, you should not sell it immediately afterward.

Today, we have a flippers economy where the sneakers and street wear shares are as valuable as that of Apple. And have even outpaced the returns at times on the S&P 500. It is wise for people to re-evaluate their strategies in the modern world of stockbrokers. When you believe that the bubble will eventually burst on the resale market, then you can treat your funds the way Jordon Belford does in "The Wolf of Wall Street" by all means. However, for those who believe that the resell market will continue to do well, then perhaps you will be wise enough to consider that $1000 right now is not as good as $20,000 down the road.

Now consider the Stayfresh account on StockX. His 2279 pairs are among the 20 most valuable collections and outdo the next closest holder by 210 pairs in volume. Although his collection on the pair is small at $212, or 41%, his strategy mirrors to that of Buffett in 2 ways. Firstly, he has diversified his account more than the others so that a single dip in the shoe price will not affect him by much. Secondly, most of his holdings are from as far back as 2008, which, in the context of sneakers, is like holding onto something since prehistoric time.

Even for the people that consider themselves as passive consumers and buy from organizations such as Netflix, Apple, and Amazon, the Buffett strategy reveals gains of $51,996, $12398, and $6628 had the person invested $1000 and held onto them for a period of ten years. In case you just value Buffett for what he is worth, you will invest in companies that you believe in and always be prepared for a long game.

The key is integrity

While attempting to evaluate the people he is going to hire, Warren Buffett points out 3 key attributes: intelligence, energy, and integrity as being the most important factors. In the super-competitive world of academics and business, the first two traits can be observed in almost 99% of the applicants. But Buffett says that integrity is not something you can decide to have on a day. It is not hard-wired in the DNA Buffett says. In case you do not wish to have it, you never will. Although it is one thing to say that you will dedicate more time and efforts to some specific task that needs finishing, it is quite another ball game to do it with strong moral principles as it might affect others adversely as well.

The true capital is knowledge

In the case of business or athletics or whatever, the rise to the top is a mixture of natural talent blended with hard work and dedication. In case winning at the stock market was just like picking a handful of companies, a person will not have to do much and then wait for 20 years, everybody would be rich. This is probably the reason crypto currencies are so popular among millennials.

For Warren Buffett, it is research on which the decision to invest in a company is based on, and he uses his massive bankroll to plant the seeds all over the place to see what grows out of them. And his secret trick? He reads and reads. He reads for at least 5-6 hours daily. Even the other luminaries such as Bill Gates and Elon Musk have all used the teachings and views of others as a major tenet in their approach to business.

Failure may be a good thing

In the HBO documentary called Becoming Warren Buffett, he has recounted his efforts of getting into Harvard Business School after he had graduated from the University of Nebraska in just 3 years. They told him that he would be interviewed around a place close to Chicago. He got there, they interviewed him for ten minutes and said forget it. You are not going to Harvard. He went to Columbia Business School instead, but it is hardly a consolation. However, the school led him to a teacher who was to prove instrumental in shaping his attitude towards investing. He was Benjamin Graham, who is regarded as the father of value investing. According to Buffett, he was an incredible teacher and a natural. He drew in all the students.

Conclusion

Warren Buffett's rules for success are a foundation in value investing. They may be open for adaptation and further interpretation going forward. It is an open discussion as to what degree you can modify the rules, considering the future. It is difficult to find consistent operating histories, and there are many intangibles that play an increasingly greater role in franchise values, and the continued blurring of boundaries between the various industries has made the business analysis even more challenging. Everybody wants to invest like Buffett, but few have managed to mimic his incredible success.

[1] Delos Santos, J. M. (2017, July 19). Bill Gates's Top 10 Rules For Success. Retrieved from https://project-management.com/bill-gates-top-10-rules-for-success/

[2] Bill Gates's Top 10 Rules For Success (@BillGates). (2015, June 27). Retrieved from https://www.youtube.com/watch?v=wq-gba5nMrc

[3] Bill Gates's Top 10 Rules For Success

[4] Delos Santos, 2017

[5] Bill Gates's Top 10 Rules For Success

[6] Bill Gates's Top 10 Rules For Success

[7] Delos Santos, 2017

[8] "Wit & Wisdom." *The Week*, no. 1001, Dennis Publishing Ltd., Dec. 2014, p. 25.

[9] *https://www.ruleoneinvesting.com/blog/how-to-invest/warren-buffett-quotes-on-investing-success/*

[10] Guenther, E. (2014). To Have Walked Far with Others. *The American Organist, 48(8),* 5.

[11] *Buffett explains how to invest in stocks when inflation spikes.*

http://www.msn.com/en-us/money/markets/buffett-explains-how-to-invest-in-stocks-when-inflation-spikes/ar-BBJ8GNj

[12] https://www.ruleoneinvesting.com/blog/how-to-invest/warren-buffett-quotes-on-investing-success/

[13] https://www.ruleoneinvesting.com/blog/how-to-invest/warren-buffett-quotes-on-investing-success/

[14] *Warren Buffett: 13 of his most brilliant quotes - Business ....* https://www.businessinsider.com/13-brilliant-quotes-from-warren-buffett-2017-8

[15] *Warren Buffett: 13 of his most brilliant quotes - Business ....* https://www.businessinsider.com/13-brilliant-quotes-from-warren-buffett-2017-8

[16] *Warren Buffet - [PDF Document].* https://vdocuments.site/documents/warren-buffet-5584502972ed7.html (https://vdocuments.site/documents/warren-buffet-5584502972ed7.html)

[17] *Warren Buffett - It takes 20 years to build a reputation ....* https://www.brainyquote.com/quotes/warren_buffett_108887

[18] *Quote by Warren Buffet: "Should you find yourself in a ....* https://www.goodreads.com/quotes/47192-should-you-find-yourself-in-a-chronically-leaking-boat-energy

[19] *https://www.ruleoneinvesting.com/blog/how-to-invest/warren-buffett-quotes-on-investing-success/*

[20] *https://www.ruleoneinvesting.com/blog/how-to-invest/warren-buffett-quotes-on-investing-success/*

[21] *Warren Buffett: 13 of his most brilliant quotes - Business https://www.businessinsider.com/13-brilliant-quotes-from-warren-buffett-2017-8*

[22] *Quote by Warren Buffet: "Should you find yourself in a https://www.goodreads.com/quotes/47192-should-you-find-yourself-in-a-chronically-leaking-boat-energy*

[23] *Warren Buffet - [PDF Document]. https://vdocuments.site/documents/warren-buffet-5584502972ed7.html* (https://vdocuments.site/documents/warren-buffet-5584502972ed7.html)

www.ingramcontent.com/pod-product-compliance
Lightning Source LLC
Chambersburg PA
CBHW021819170526
45157CB00007B/2652